JULES VERNE

Jules Gabriel Verne (1828–1905) was a French novelist, playwright and poet. His most famous works are *Around the World in Eighty Days* (1873), *Journey to the Centre of the Earth* (1864), and *Twenty Thousand Leagues Under the Sea* (1869).

Often referred to as the 'Father of Science Fiction', Verne's interest in travel and adventure grew from a childhood spent in the busy maritime port of Nantes, France. From there he was sent to study law in Paris where he would eventually set up his own practice in 1850. It was during this time that his attention turned towards the theatre and, encouraged by his friend Alexander Dumas, he began writing numerous plays and operettas, eventually leaving the law to set up his own theatre company.

He began writing novels soon after. His first published book, *Le Salon de 1857*, was published that same year and began a period where Verne and his wife sailed the British Isles, providing the emerging novelist with material for his stories. Over the next decade he would write many of his classic novels. He published three books in 1864 alone and, despite having frequent trouble with publishers and struggling to support his family, he remained incredibly prolific throughout this period.

His stories feature numerous inventions that are still considered well ahead of their time, such as the submarine, deep-sea exploration and space travel. He remains the second most translated writer of all time after Agatha Christie.

LAURA EASON

Laura Eason is the author of twenty plays, original works and adaptations, a musical-book writer and a screenwriter. Selected productions include: *Sex with Strangers* (more than twenty productions in the US and internationally including Second Stage, NYC; Signature Theatre, DC; Steppenwolf Theatre, Chicago; Geffen Playhouse, LA; Sydney Theatre, AU; Blackwing Productions, Buenos Aires, Argentina; published by Overlook Press and DPS); *The Undeniable Sound of Right Now* (Rattlestick Theatre and Women's Project Theatre, NYC); *The Adventures of Tom Sawyer* (Hartford Stage, CT; Actors Theatre, KY; Denver Center, People's Light, PA; St. Louis Rep, published by DPS), and *Around the World in 80 Days* (New Vic and Royal Exchange, UK; Lookingglass Theatre, Chicago; Baltimore Centerstage; published by Broadway Play Publishing and Nick Hern Books). She wrote the book for the musicals *Days Like Today*, music and lyrics by Alan Schmuckler (Writers Theatre, Chicago) and *Summerland,* music by Jenny Giering, lyrics by Sean Barry (Chicago Shakespeare Theatre commission). As a screenwriter, Laura wrote for seasons two, three and four of the Netflix's drama *House of Cards* (WGA nomination for Outstanding Achievement in Drama Series). She is an Ensemble Member and the former Artistic Director of Chicago's Lookingglass Theatre (2011 Regional Tony Award). In New York, she is a member of Rising Phoenix Rep, New Georges, and a Women's Project Playwright's Lab alumna. More information at lauraeason.com or @LeasonNYC.

JULES VERNE'S

AROUND THE WORLD

IN 80 DAYS

ADAPTED BY
LAURA EASON

NICK HERN BOOKS
London
www.nickhernbooks.co.uk

A Nick Hern Book

This stage adaptation of *Around the World in 80 Days* first published in Great Britain as a paperback original in 2014 by Nick Hern Books Limited, The Glasshouse, 49a Goldhawk Road, London W12 8QP

Reprinted with a new cover in 2017

Cover image: designed by Bob King Creative; photography by Steve Tanner
Designed and typeset by Nick Hern Books, London
Printed in Great Britain by Mimeo Ltd, Huntingdon, Cambridgeshire PE29 6XX

A CIP catalogue record for this book is available from the British Library

ISBN 978 1 84842 517 0

Woodland CARBON
www.woodlandcarbon.co.uk
NICK HERN BOOKS
Printed on Carbon Captured paper

Around the World in 80 Days was commissioned and first presented in the United States of America by Lookingglass Theater Company, Chicago (David Catlin, Artistic Director; Philip R Smith, Producing Artistic Director; Heidi Stillman, Artistic Director of New Work; Rachel E Kraft, Executive Director), and opened on 27 April 2008 at the Lookingglass Theater. The cast, in alphabetical order, were as follows:

CAPTAIN SPEEDY	Rom Barkhordar
MRS AOUDA	Ravi Batista
INSPECTOR FIX	Joe Dempsey
PASSEPARTOUT	Kevin Douglas
MR NAIDU	Anish Jethmalami
CAPTAIN VON DARIUS	Ericka Ratcliffe
COLONEL STAMP PROCTOR	Nick Sandys
PHILEAS FOGG	Philip R Smith

Other parts played by members of the company.

Director	Laura Eason
Set Designer	Jacqueline and Richard Penrod
Costume Designer	Mara Blumenfeld
Lighting Designer	Lee Keenan
Sound Designer	Joshua Horvath
Composer	Kevin O'Donnell
Choreographer and Movement Director	Tracy Walsh
Fight Choreographer	Nick Sandys
Props Designer	Stephanie Barkley and Galen Pejeau
Production Stage Manager	Sara Gmitter
Assistant Stage Manager	Jonathan Templeton
Dramaturgs	Margot Bordelon and Cassandra Sanders
Director of Production	Alexandra Blunt

Around the World in 80 Days received its London premiere at the St. James Theatre on 26 November 2015. The cast for the London production was as follows:

PHILEAS FOGG	Robert Portal
PASSEPARTOUT	Simon Gregor
INSPECTOR FIX	Tony Gardner
MRS AOUDA	Shanaya Rafaat
COLONEL PROCTOR	Tim Steed
MR NAIDU	Eben Figueiredo
MISS SINGH	Lena Kaur
JUDGE OBADIAH	Liz Sutherland

Other parts played by members of the company.

Director	Lucy Bailey
Designer	Anna Fleischle
Composer	Django Bates
Movement Director	Lizzi Gee
Lighting Designer	Chris Davey
Sound Designer	Mic Pool
Producers	Simon Friend Entertainment
	St. James Theatre Productions
	Ros Povey Productions
Associate Producer	JAM Pictures

The first performance of this production of *Around the World in 80 Days* took place at the New Vic Theatre, Newcastle-under-Lyme, on 23 June 2017, in partnership with New Vic Theatre, Simon Friend and Kenny Wax Family Entertainment and in association with the Royal Exchange Theatre, Manchester.

The production was based on the New Vic Theatre production of *Around the World in 80 Days* which opened at New Vic Theatre on 19 April 2013 and was revived again on 20 June 2014 in collaboration with the Royal Exchange Theatre, Manchester. The cast for the 2017 production was as follows:

MR NAIDU	Pushpinder Chani
CAPTAIN SPEEDY	Simi Egbejumi-David
MRS AOUDA	Kirsten Foster
COLONEL PROCTOR	Matthew Ganley
INSPECTOR FIX	Dennis Herdman
PASSEPARTOUT	Michael Hugo
MISS SINGH	Joey Parsad
PHILEAS FOGG	Andrew Pollard
UNDERSTUDY/ASM	Jessica Lucia Andrade
UNDERSTUDY/ASM	Stefan Ruiz

Director	Theresa Heskins
Designer	Lis Evans
Composer	James Atherton
Movement Director	Beverley Norris Edmunds
Lighting Designer	Alexandra Stafford
Sound Designer	James Earls-Davis
Associate Sound Designer	Alex Day
Casting Director	Anji Carroll CDG
Assistant Director	Eleanor Clare Taylor
Vocal Coach	Mark Langley

Set, made props and costumes all by New Vic Theatre workshop and costume departments. With thanks to all staff at New Vic Theatre and production and technical teams both at the New Vic and on tour. Special thanks to previous cast members Suzanne Ahmet, Okorie Chukwu, Matt Connor, Rebecca Grant, Susan Hingley and Matt Rixon.

Characters

PHILEAS FOGG, *a man about forty years of age, tall,*
handsome, calm and unresponsive to what might normally
excite interest or emotion. Seen in the various phases of his
daily life as perfectly well-balanced and as exactly regulated
as a chronometer
PASSEPARTOUT, *a true Parisian and former circus performer.*
He's playful and honest with an adventurous nature he is
trying to squash
INSPECTOR FIX, *an overeager inspector from Scotland Yard*
who mistakes Fogg for a bank robber he is after
MRS AOUDA, *a well-educated, self-possessed, beautiful*
widow who joins Fogg and Passepartout on their journey
after they rescue her from near-death in India

Plus, in alphabetical order

AMERICAN TRAIN PORTER
ANGRY MALABAR MEN
AOUDA GUARDS
BATULCAR
BEGGAR WOMAN
BOMBAY CONSUL
CALCUTTA POLICEMAN
CAPTAIN BLOSSOM VON DARIUS
CAPTAIN SPEEDY
CARNATIC PURSER
CIRCUS PERFORMERS
CLERK
CLUB MAN
COLONEL STAMP PROCTOR
ENGINEER *on* The Henrietta
MR FLANAGAN
FLOWER-SELLER
GENERAL GRANT PASSENGERS

GENERAL GRANT PURSER
HENRIETTA CREWMEN
HONG KONG CONSUL
JAMES, *Fogg's valet*
JUDGE OBADAIAH
LIVERPOOL POLICEMAN
LUIGI *the circus performer*
MISS SINGH
MONGOLIA PASSENGERS
MONGOLIA PURSER
MR MUDGE
MR NAIDU
OPIUM SMOKERS
PENINSULA CONDUCTOR
MR RALPH
RANGOON PASSENGER
SAILOR
STREET-SWEEP
MR STUART
SUEZ CONSUL
TRAIN BANDITS

Suggested Doubling for a Cast of Eight

PHILEAS FOGG

PASSEPARTOUT

INSPECTOR FIX, *also plays* CLUB MAN

MRS AOUDA, *also plays* BEGGAR WOMAN

MR NAIDU (ENSEMBLE #1), *also plays* JAMES, MR RALPH, OPIUM DENIZEN, LUIGI, RANGOON PASSENGER, TRAIN BANDIT, GENERAL GRANT PASSENGER, MR MUDGE, HENRIETTA CREWMAN, LIVERPOOL POLICEMAN

COLONEL STAMP PROCTOR (ENSEMBLE #2), *also plays* MR STUART, MONGOLIA PURSER, ANGRY MALABAR MAN, AOUDA GUARD, JUDGE OBADAIAH, HONG KONG CONSUL, CIRCUS PERFORMER, CARNATIC PURSER, GENERAL GRANT PURSER, ENGINEER

CAPTAIN BLOSSOM VON DARIUS (ENSEMBLE #3), *also plays* FLOWER-SELLER, SUEZ CONSUL, MONGOLIA PASSENGER, ANGRY MALABAR MAN, MISS SINGH, CLERK, OPIUM DENIZEN, CIRCUS PERFORMER, GENERAL GRANT PASSENGER, AMERICAN TRAIN PORTER, SAILOR, HENRIETTA CREWMAN

CAPTAIN SPEEDY (ENSEMBLE #4), *also plays* STREET-SWEEP, MR FLANAGAN, MONGOLIA PASSENGER, ANGRY MALABAR MAN, BOMBAY CONSUL, PENINSULA CONDUCTOR, AOUDA GUARD, CALCUTTA POLICEMAN, OPIUM DENIZEN, BATULCAR, GENERAL GRANT PASSENGER, TRAIN BANDIT

Setting

Time: The 30th of September to the 22nd of December, 1872.

Locations: London, Suez, Bombay, Calcutta, Singapore, Hong Kong, Yokohama, the plains of the American West and New York City.

Set: The set is an open, flexible environment that can transform into a multitude of locations, around the world and back again, at lightning speed. All locations should be set simply and suggestively, not realised in full detail. To help follow the journey, perhaps there is a map of the world somewhere onstage.

Sound and Music: The sound design can be an aid in charting the journey and, ideally, there is original music and/or sound through much of the play.

Big Numbers: There are nine 'numbers' in the show including: 'A Day in the Life', 'The Journey Begins', 'The Red Sea Number', 'An Elephant Chase', 'The Tea Dance', 'A Circus Act', 'Bandits Attack the Train', 'Sledge Ride' and 'A Storm at Sea'.

ACT ONE

Scene One

Phileas Fogg

Lights up.

Big Number – 'A Day in the Life':

Day 1: Morning in London, Monday September 30th, 1872.

Out of bed rises PHILEAS FOGG, *handsome, around forty, a man so precise that to say his life runs like clockwork is no exaggeration.*

In a movement sequence we see FOGG's *very regimented routine:*

   – Wakes up.

   – Stretches and touches his toes.

   – Puts on his suit coat.

   – Has tea and toast delivered by his valet JAMES.

   – Gets his hat and walking cane.

JAMES. Good day, Mr Fogg.

FOGG. Good day.

   – Exits his home.

   – Arrives on the street.

BEGGAR WOMAN. Alms for the poor?

   – Gives money to the BEGGAR WOMAN.

Thank you, Mr Fogg.

   – Walks down the road.

FOGG (*to* FLOWER-SELLER). Good day.

– *Takes a flower from the* FLOWER-SELLER *for his lapel.*

– *Nods and walks on as she says:*

FLOWER-SELLER. Good day, Mr Fogg.

– *Arrives at the Reform Club.*

– *Plays whist with one other* GENTLEMAN.

– *Wins at whist.*

– *Collects his winnings into a little purse.*

FOGG (*to* GENTLEMAN). Good evening.

GENTLEMAN. Good evening.

– *Begins his walk home.*

FOGG (*to* FLOWER-SELLER). Good evening.

FLOWER-SELLER. Good evening, Mr Fogg.

– *Arrives at home.*

– *Gives his coat, hat and cane to his valet* JAMES.

JAMES. Goodnight, Mr Fogg.

FOGG. Goodnight.

– *Sighs.*

– *Goes to sleep.*

A moment of silence.

Day 2: Morning in London, Tuesday October 1st, 1872.

The day in the life pattern begins to repeat. Although everything around FOGG *is slightly different,* FOGG *is exactly the same in every movement, action and gesture.*

In movement, FOGG *once again:*

– *Wakes up.*

– *Stretches and touches his toes.*

– *Puts on his suit coat.*

– Has tea and toast delivered by his valet JAMES.

– Gets his hat and walking cane.

JAMES. Good day, Mr Fogg.

FOGG. Good day.

– Exits his home.

– Arrives on the street.

BEGGAR WOMAN. Alms for the poor?

– Gives money to the BEGGAR WOMAN.

Thank you, Mr Fogg.

– Walks down the road.

FOGG (*to* FLOWER-SELLER). Good day.

– Takes a flower from the FLOWER-SELLER *for his lapel.*

– Nods and walks on as she says:

FLOWER-SELLER. Good day, Mr Fogg.

As the sequence continues, we see a STREET-SWEEP *approach the* FLOWER-SELLER. *As they talk, the movement sequence continues in its regular pattern.*

STREET-SWEEP. So, that's Mr Phileas Fogg, is it?

FLOWER-SELLER. Cuts quite a figure, eh?

Movement sequence continues under dialogue as FOGG:

– Arrives at the Reform Club.

– Plays whist with one other GENTLEMAN.

STREET-SWEEP. Must be a wealthy man.

FLOWER-SELLER. Undoubtedly. But no one knows how he made his fortune and, from what I'm told, Mr Fogg never speaks of it himself.

Movement sequence continues under dialogue as FOGG:

– Wins at whist.

– Collects his winnings into a little purse.

FOGG (*to* GENTLEMAN). Good evening.

GENTLEMAN. Good evening.

   – Begins his walk home.

STREET-SWEEP. Generous?

FLOWER-SELLER. Not lavish but when money is needed for a noble or useful cause, he seems to supply it quietly.

STREET-SWEEP. On the town much, is he?

FLOWER-SELLER. No, keeps to himself, hasn't any family or friends beyond his whist partners at the club. But a fine fellow is Mr Fogg!

   FOGG *passes them.*

   Good evening, Mr Fogg.

FOGG. Good evening.

   FOGG *walks on. They watch him go.*

FLOWER-SELLER (*to* STREET-SWEEP). Well, goodnight.

STREET-SWEEP (*tipping his hat to her*). Goodnight.

   Movement sequence continues as FOGG:

   – Arrives at home.

   – Gives his coat, hat and cane to his valet JAMES.

JAMES. Goodnight, Mr Fogg.

FOGG. Goodnight.

   – Sighs.

   – Goes to sleep.

   A moment of silence.

Day 3: Morning in London, Wednesday October 2nd, 1872.

The day in the life pattern begins to repeat.

In movement sequence, FOGG *once again:*

   – Wakes up.

– Stretches and touches his toes.

– Puts on his suit coat.

– Has tea and toast delivered by his valet JAMES.

At the moment FOGG's *lips touch the tea everything comes to a screeching halt.*

FOGG. James – the temperature of the tea. It is not at the required ninety-seven degrees.

JAMES. Terribly sorry, sir. (*Knowing he's done for.*) I expect that's it for me, then. Shall I place an advertisement for a new man before I go?

FOGG (*calmly, quickly*). If you would.

Movement sequence continues as FOGG:

– Gets his hat and walking cane.

(*To* JAMES.) Good luck.

JAMES. Goodbye. (*Exits in resignation.*)

– Exits his home.

Scene Two

Passepartout Finds a Comfortable Position

Movement sequence continues as FOGG:

– Arrives on the street.

PASSEPARTOUT *enters. He is French and a former circus performer. He approaches the* FLOWER-SELLER.

PASSEPARTOUT. Excuse me, I'm looking for Number Seven, Savile Row, Mr Phileas Fogg's residence?

FLOWER-SELLER. He's just behind you, love.

PASSEPARTOUT. *Merci!*

PASSEPARTOUT *walks to* FOGG's *house.*

Movement sequence continues:

BEGGAR WOMAN. Alms for the poor?

– *Gives money to the* BEGGAR WOMAN.

Thank you, Mr Fogg.

– *Walks down the road.*

FOGG *is intercepted by* PASSEPARTOUT, *but continues his usual route as they talk.*

PASSEPARTOUT. Excuse me… Mr Fogg?

FOGG. Yes, I am he.

PASSEPARTOUT. I have come about your advertisement for a new valet.

FOGG (*unfazed*). That was quick. Well, have you recommendations?

PASSEPARTOUT *hands* FOGG *a document.* FOGG *scan it.*

PASSEPARTOUT. My name is Jean but they call me Passepartout, which roughly translated, *monsieur*, means I have a knack of slipping out of tricky situations!

FOGG *passes the* FLOWER-SELLER *and gets the flower for his lapel.*

FLOWER-SELLER. Good day, Mr Fogg.

FOGG (*to* FLOWER-SELLER). Good day. (*To* PASSEPARTOUT.) A Frenchman?

PASSEPARTOUT. Yes, *monsieur* – a Parisian through and through! I have been a singer, horse rider, trapeze artist, tightrope walker and… a goat herder. There never was a man more curious about the world than I.

FOGG. I see.

PASSEPARTOUT. But having heard, *monsieur*, that you are the most exact and settled gentleman in the United Kingdom, I have come in the hope of living with you a tranquil life and forgetting even the name of Passepartout.

FOGG *hands* PASSEPARTOUT *back his document.*

FOGG. You are well recommended. You know my conditions?

PASSEPARTOUT. Yes, *monsieur*.

FOGG. Good! From this moment onwards, you are in my service. What time is it?

PASSEPARTOUT *takes out a silver pocket watch and* FOGG *compares it to his.*

PASSEPARTOUT. Twenty-two minutes after three.

FOGG. You are thirty seconds too slow.

PASSEPARTOUT. But this was my great-grandfather's watch and –

FOGG. No matter. It's enough to mention the error. I shall return to my home at Number Seven Savile Row tonight at exactly nine fifty-eight p.m. and will retire at exactly ten fifty-nine.

FOGG *hands him a set of keys.*

Good day, Passepartout.

PASSEPARTOUT. Good day, sir.

FOGG *goes into the club.* PASSEPARTOUT *makes his way back to the house, passing the* FLOWER-SELLER.

FLOWER-SELLER. How did it go, then?

PASSEPARTOUT. I've seen wax figures at Madame Tussaud's more lively than him! But, I'm his new valet. And as I yearn for a quiet life, we shall get on together, Mr Fogg and I!

Scene Three

A Bet is Made at the Reform Club

FOGG *moves to the whist game with his usual partners, all rich and highly respectable men.* FOGG *sits opposite* MR STUART *and* MR FLANAGAN *sits opposite* MR RALPH.

FLANAGAN. Well, Ralph, what's the latest on the robbery at your bank?

STUART. What's this now?

FLANAGAN. Didn't you hear? A thief made off with fifty-five thousand pounds from the Bank of England!

STUART. Fifty-five thousand pounds!

FLANAGAN. Quite a fortune!

RALPH. Without a doubt, the thief will be caught!

STUART. No, I say the chances are in favour of the thief.

RALPH. How? Where can he go? No country is safe for him.

STUART. Oh, I don't know about that – the world is big enough.

FOGG. It was once.

FOGG *sets the shuffled deck in front of* STUART.

(*To* STUART, *re: the cards.*) Cut, sir.

STUART *cuts the cards.*

STUART. What do you mean by 'once'? Has the world grown smaller?

FOGG. Indeed, it has. (*To* FLANAGAN.) The cards, sir.

FLANAGAN *deals.*

RALPH. I agree with Mr Fogg – the world *has* grown smaller, since a man can now go round it ten times faster than a hundred years ago.

FLANAGAN. That is why the search for the thief is likely to succeed.

STUART. No, that is why the thief will likely get away. So, Ralph, you maintain that because you can now go round the world in three months –

FOGG. Eighty days.

STUART. Fogg, for a man who never leaves London, you know the geography of the world with more familiarity than any man I've ever met.

FLANAGAN. Fogg is right, Stuart, to travel the world in eighty days is possible now that the final section of the Great Indian Peninsula Railway has been opened.

STUART. You may be right theoretically, Mr Fogg, but not practically.

FOGG. Practically also, Mr Stuart.

All the MEN *pick up their cards except* STUART, *who glares at* FOGG.

Be so good as to play.

STUART *picks up his cards and the* MEN *begin to play.*

STUART. But eighty days doesn't take into account bad weather, shipwrecks, railway accidents and so on.

FOGG. All included.

STUART. But suppose bandits pull up the rails, stop the train, pillage the luggage vans and kidnap the passengers!?

FOGG. All included.

STUART. No, it's impossible!

FOGG. On the contrary, quite possible. Your turn, Flanagan.

STUART. I would wager five thousand pounds that it isn't!

FOGG. Wager whatever you like, it remains a mathematical fact.

STUART. Well, why don't you try it, then!

FOGG. A journey round the world in eighty days?

STUART. Yes.

FOGG. I should like nothing better.

STUART. When?

FOGG. At once.

STUART. I will wager ten thousand pounds that you will not succeed, Mr Fogg!

RALPH/FLANAGAN (*in shock at the size of the sum*). Ten thousand!

STUART. And it shall be the easiest money I've ever come by!

FLANAGAN. Calm yourself, my dear Stuart. It's only a joke.

STUART. When I say I'll wager, I mean it!

FOGG. I will see your wager and raise it to twenty thousand pounds.

RALPH. Twenty thousand pounds!?

FLANAGAN. Twenty thousand pounds!?

STUART. Twenty thousand pounds which you will lose by an accidental delay of even a single day? You are joking!

FOGG. A true Englishman never jokes when he is talking about a wager.

FLANAGAN. But, Mr Fogg, eighty days is the estimate of the *least* possible time in which the journey can be made.

FOGG. A well-used minimum suffices for everything.

RALPH. But, in order to meet it, you must jump with mathematical precision from trains to steamers and from steamers to trains.

FOGG. Then with mathematical precision I will jump!

The game halts.

The wager is now twenty thousand pounds. Do you accept it, gentlemen?

FLANAGAN *begs off.* STUART *and* RALPH *talk briefly and look to* FOGG.

STUART/RALPH. We do.

FOGG. A train leaves for Dover at a quarter after nine. I shall be on it.

STUART. Tonight?!

FOGG. Tonight.

FLANAGAN/RALPH. Tonight?!

FOGG. As today is Wednesday, the 2nd of October, I shall be due in London, in this very room of the Reform Club, on Saturday the 21st of December at exactly...

The clock begins to chime nine p.m.

Nine p.m. You will examine my passport and be able to judge whether I have accomplished the journey agreed upon.

FOGG *looks to* STUART *and* RALPH.

If I have, you two gentlemen will each owe me ten thousand pounds. If I have not, my twenty thousand pounds will belong to you, in fact and in right.

STUART/RALPH. Indeed.

FOGG. Then the bet is made.

FOGG *lays down his cards.*

Diamonds are trumps.

FOGG *gathers his winnings.*

And with that, I take my leave. Good evening.

STUART/RALPH/FLANAGAN. Good evening.

FOGG *makes his way home. The* GENTLEMAN *sit, stunned.*

STUART. Is it possible? Has Phileas Fogg really made such a foolish wager on this impossible journey?

RALPH. That's got to be *half* his fortune.

FLANAGAN. I bet you both a thousand pounds he makes it back in time!

STUART. Two to one he won't!

A CLUB MAN *approaches.*

CLUB MAN. What's the bet, gents?

FLANAGAN. Whether Phileas Fogg can make it around the world in eighty days. I say he will!

CLUB MAN. Certainly not! I bet you a thousand he won't!

STUART. Without question, Fogg will fail!

MEN *gather around and throw money down for and against* FOGG.

Scene Four

The Departure

FOGG's *house*. PASSEPARTOUT *sits contentedly on his bed next to a glowing gas lamp*.

PASSEPARTOUT. Now, Jean, say *adieu* to adventure, foreign lands and the call of the unknown! A quiet life within these four walls will be all the journey you need for the rest of your life!

FOGG. Passepartout!

FOGG *has arrived home*. PASSEPARTOUT *looks with confusion at his watch*.

(*Again, not raising his voice*.) Passepartout!

PASSEPARTOUT *rushes to* FOGG.

PASSEPARTOUT. Uh... yes, *monsieur*.

FOGG. I've called you twice.

PASSEPARTOUT. I'm sorry, sir, but –

FOGG. We start for Dover and Calais in ten minutes, so we haven't a moment to lose.

PASSEPARTOUT. *Monsieur* is... going somewhere?

FOGG. Yes. We are going round the world.

PASSEPARTOUT. Round the world!?

FOGG. In eighty days. I have wagered my word and half my
     fortune that I shall make the journey in time. Don't worry
     about the trunks, we'll take only two carpet bags with the
     bare essentials and buy whatever we need along the way.
     We've only three minutes before we must leave for the
     station, so I suggest you make haste!

     PASSEPARTOUT *rushes around packing as* FOGG *calmly
     and quietly retrieves a huge roll of Bank of England notes.*

PASSEPARTOUT (*to himself*). Around the world in eighty
     days! No. This must be a joke! Perhaps we will go to Dover,
     maybe even on to Paris but no further than that!

FOGG. Make sure to bring the *Bradshaw Guide*. It's bound in
     red. It contains the timetables of every steamer and railway
     in the world.

     PASSEPARTOUT *grabs the* Bradshaw *and carries it along
     with two carpet bags. He meets* FOGG *at the door.*

     You have forgotten nothing?

PASSEPARTOUT. Nothing, *monsieur*.

     FOGG *takes one of the carpet bags, opens it, and slips into it
     the large roll of Bank of England notes.*

FOGG. Good! Take good care of that bag. There are now
     twenty thousand pounds in it.

     They exit the house.

PASSEPARTOUT (*a cry of despair*). Ahh!

FOGG. What's the matter?

PASSEPARTOUT. In my hurry, I forgot to turn off the gas lamp
     in my room!

FOGG. An unfortunate oversight, my dear fellow. You
     understand it will burn at your expense.

PASSEPARTOUT. Yes, *monsieur*.

FOGG. We are off.

Big Number – 'The Journey Begins': a huge map on the wall is revealed and a small train is placed on it. The train begins to trace FOGG's *journey along the map. In image, we see a suggestion of* FOGG *and* PASSEPARTOUT *riding on a train. The train is then replaced by a boat on the map. In image, we see a suggestion of* FOGG *and* PASSEPARTOUT *riding on a boat. The boat is replaced by a train on the map. In image, we see a suggestion of* FOGG *and* PASSEPARTOUT *riding on a train. The sound of a train whistle blows and, in image, we see a suggestion of* FOGG *and* PASSEPARTOUT *exiting a train.*

Scene Five

Brindisi

FOGG *and* PASSEPARTOUT *are walking off a train.*

FOGG. Arrival in Brindisi, Italy, on schedule.

PASSEPARTOUT. I'm beginning to believe, sir, you really do have the intention of going around the world.

FOGG (*consulting the* Bradshaw Guide). From London to Dover, Dover to Calais, Calais to Brindisi, Brindisi to Suez, Suez to Bombay, Bombay to Calcutta, Calcutta to Hong Kong, Hong Kong to Yokohama, Yokohama to San Francisco, San Francisco to New York, New York to Liverpool, Liverpool to London. By… rail, steamboat, rail, steamer, rail, steamer, steamer, rail, steamer, steamer, steamer and, finally, rail. Total eighty days.

A steamboat whistle blows.

Come along, we've only a hour to catch *The Mongolia.*

PASSEPARTOUT. *The MONGOLIA, monsieur?*

FOGG. A fine steamer bound for Bombay via Suez.

PASSEPARTOUT (*delighted and excited*). Bombay!? (*Catching himself.*) Won't care for it!

Transition: on the map, the little train is replaced by a boat, showing FOGG *sailing over the ocean to Suez. In image, we see a suggestion of* FOGG *and* PASSEPARTOUT *on a boat.*

Scene Six

Inspector Fix in Suez

The British Consulate office in Suez. INSPECTOR FIX *reads a British newspaper as the* SUEZ CONSUL, *wearing a very distinctive hat, works in frustration as* FIX *chatters at him.*

SUEZ CONSUL. How long do you think you'll be here in Suez, Inspector Fix?

FIX. Until the thief of the Bank of England is caught! A man can't just abscond with fifty-five thousand pounds and expect to get away with it.

SUEZ CONSUL. But it seems as though he has.

FIX. Well, Scotland Yard has sent the best men, as well as myself, to all the main British ports. It won't be long before we capture the rogue.

SUEZ CONSUL. I do hope you find him *soon*, Inspector.

FIX. As do I... for there is a reward of two thousand pounds!

The SUEZ CONSUL *sighs at the prospect of* FIX *being in Suez for a long time.* FIX *looks at the newspaper.*

Have you heard about this Phileas Fogg attempting to go around the world in eighty days?

SUEZ CONSUL. Yes, Inspector.

FIX. He's a lunatic! And travelling in the winter, too, at the mercy of the snow and ice? Why, even the best ocean steamers often run two or three days behind time in winter, isn't that right?

SUEZ CONSUL. Yes, Inspector.

FIX (*re: the paper*). Now! Just a moment! Here's a description of this Mr Fogg. It matches the description of our bank robber exactly!

SUEZ CONSUL (*looking at the paper*). I don't know – that description could be almost any one.

FIX. Oh, no, that's the man! Who else would bet twenty thousand pounds simply to prove a point? Only a madman or a thief would risk his fortune for his word!

SUEZ CONSUL. But, Inspector, surely you don't think –

FIX. If he's making his way around the world, he'd have to come here, through the Suez Canal, on his way to Bombay, isn't that right?

SUEZ CONSUL. Yes, but hundreds of men pass through Suez every day –

FIX. Oh, I will keep my eye out for this man! And if I'm the one to catch him, my future is made!

SUEZ CONSUL. But how will you ever know Mr Fogg when you see him?

FIX. A man rather feels the presence of these fellows, Consul. You must have a sense for them – a sixth sense – as I do. I've arrested more than one of these 'gentlemen' in my time, and, if he's the man, he'll not slip through my fingers.

The SUEZ CONSUL *and* FIX *look up to see* FOGG *and* PASSEPARTOUT *standing before them.*

FOGG (*to* FIX). Morning.

FIX (*to* FOGG). Morning.

FOGG (*to* SUEZ CONSUL). Would you be so kind as to stamp our passports?

SUEZ CONSUL. Of course, sir.

PASSEPARTOUT *hands the* SUEZ CONSUL *their passports. The* SUEZ CONSUL *looks from the passports to* FOGG.

You are Mr Phileas Fogg?

FOGG. I am.

FIX, *stunned, tries to make himself inconspicuous, and spies at* FOGG *from behind his newspaper.*

SUEZ CONSUL. And this man is your valet, Mr Passepartout?

FOGG. Yes.

SUEZ CONSUL. And you are going…?

FOGG. To Bombay.

SUEZ CONSUL. Very good, sir. But as an Englishman, with this territory being under British rule, no passport is required.

FOGG. Certainly, Consul, but I wish to prove that I came through Suez.

SUEZ CONSUL. Very well.

The SUEZ CONSUL *stamps their passports.*

Enjoy your trip.

FOGG. Thank you. Good day.

FOGG *and* PASSEPARTOUT *step out of the office.* FIX *rushes to the door and watches them.*

PASSEPARTOUT. We have a few hours before the boat launches, *monsieur*, if you would like to look around…?

FOGG. I believe I've seen it all in the *Journal of the Royal Geographical Society*. And I've an appointment for whist with some gentlemen on the boat.

FOGG *pulls out the roll of banknotes and hands some to* PASSEPARTOUT.

Please go and make our purchases. Then, you are free to see the sights as you please.

PASSEPARTOUT. Thank you, *monsieur*, but, from my days with the circus, I've already seen more of the world than I ever plan to again. I'll see you on the ship shortly.

FOGG *and* PASSEPARTOUT *part ways. Focus shifts back to* FIX *and the* SUEZ CONSUL.

FIX. 'Enjoy your trip'?!

SUEZ CONSUL. He seems like a nice enough fellow –

FIX. Did you see that roll of banknotes?! No! That is the thief of the Bank of England!

SUEZ CONSUL. But, Inspector, isn't it awfully strange that a thief being sought around the globe would choose have his passport stamped when he's not obliged to?

FIX. No! That's our man! I can't let him get away! I will board *The Mongolia* and have Scotland Yard send on a warrant for Fogg's arrest. I will have him in hand when we arrive in Bombay!

Transition: The boat on the map continues to travel.

Scene Seven

On *The Mongolia*

PASSEPARTOUT *is standing with* FOGG *on the deck of* The Mongolia, *along with other international* PASSENGERS *who look out to the water.*

PASSEPARTOUT. So, we just left Suez?

FOGG. Yes.

PASSEPARTOUT. In Egypt?

FOGG. Yes, in Egypt.

PASSEPARTOUT. On the continent of Africa?

FOGG. Yes.

PASSEPARTOUT. And now we sail across the Red Sea...

FOGG. To the Arabian Sea.

PASSEPARTOUT. To India.

FOGG. Indeed.

PASSEPARTOUT (*thrilled*). The Red Sea! (*Explaining*.) With the circus, I saw the whole of Europe many times over but never did I think I'd – (*Catching himself*.) wish so much to be at home. In bed. Quietly staring at the ceiling.

The MONGOLIA PURSER *returns and speaks to all the people on the deck.*

MONGOLIA PURSER (*in Italian*). *Signori e signore belle, è tempo per un ballo romantico.* [It's time for dancing on the deck!]

Big Number – 'The Red Sea Number': two couples begin to dance, it is lovely and playfully romantic. FIX, trying badly to mix in with the crowd, accidentally gets caught up in the dance.

When the dance is over, PASSEPARTOUT *is overcome with emotion.*

PASSEPARTOUT. Who could imagine something so delightful!

FOGG. Time for whist.

As FOGG *exits, he is greeted by another passenger,* MR NAIDU, *and Indian businessman.*

MR NAIDU. Mr Fogg, I enjoyed our game of whist last evening.

FOGG. Well, please join us again tonight, Mr Naidu.

MR NAIDU. It would be my pleasure.

FOGG and MR NAIDU *head off. FIX approaches* PASSEPARTOUT.

FIX. Have you the time, my good fellow?

PASSEPARTOUT. *Mais oui!*

PASSEPARTOUT *shows* FIX *his watch.*

FIX. Sir, your watch must be slow. What time are you keeping?

PASSEPARTOUT. Why, London time, of course!

FIX. But you must set your watch to the local time in each country or you will be confused.

PASSEPARTOUT. Alter my great-grandfather's watch? Never!

FIX. Well, then, it will not agree with the sun.

PASSEPARTOUT. Well, then, the sun will be wrong!

PASSEPARTOUT *begins to walk away. FIX runs around him, stopping him.*

FIX. My name is Fix. I'm in... (*Searching lamely for a cover story.*) shipping... with the... Peninsular Navigation Company.

PASSEPARTOUT. You can call me Passepartout. I work for Mr Phileas Fogg.

FIX. The gentleman who is so fond of whist?

PASSEPARTOUT. The very one.

FIX. Have you made this trip to Bombay before?

PASSEPARTOUT. No. I always wanted to see India... (*Catching himself.*) Until I decided I didn't. Too... *large* a country to be interesting, I'm sure.

FIX. No, Mr Passepartout, it is a *most* interesting place – mosques, minarets, pagodas, tigers, snakes, elephants! Exciting stuff!

PASSEPARTOUT. I've quite enough excitement as it is, jumping from steamers to trains, and from trains to steamers, trying to tour the world in eighty days!

FIX. So, it is true, what I've heard, about your Mr Fogg's attempt to circle the globe?!

PASSEPARTOUT (*excitedly*). Yes! (*Catching himself.*) Unfortunately.

FIX. He must be very rich?

PASSEPARTOUT. Well, he is carrying an enormous sum of banknotes with him.

FIX. I see. Well, come, my good Mr Passepartout. They serve Abre on board. It's a special drink you must try. You can tell me all about your travels and your intriguing Mr Fogg!

PASSEPARTOUT. Thank you, Mr Fix, I will! (*Catching himself.*) But just a simple glass of wine – I need nothing more!

Scene Eight

Back at the Reform Club

STUART *talks with* FLANAGAN *at the Reform Club.*

STUART (*laughing, delighted*). Not even twenty days into his journey and Fogg is done for!

FLANAGAN. Whatever do you mean, Stuart?

STUART. A warrant for his arrest has been sent for from India!

FLANAGAN. You don't say!

STUART. Scotland Yard believes Fogg is the thief of the Bank of England!

FLANAGAN. Oh, how absurd!

STUART. Is it? No! Fogg made this foolish wager for no other reason than to flee the country while throwing the police off his tracks!

FLANAGAN. Three to one Fogg is found innocent *and* makes it back to the Reform Club on time!

STUART. It's a bet!

FLANAGAN *and* STUART *shake.*

FLANAGAN. Fogg must now be the most traded commodity in all of England!

Scene Nine

Bombay

The sounds of a steam-engine whistle. FOGG *and*
PASSEPARTOUT, *followed by* MR NAIDU, *step out and
look around.*

FOGG. Arrival in Bombay, noon, October 20th. A gain, due to
following winds, of two days.

PASSEPARTOUT. *Mon Dieu!* There are so many people!

FOGG. One hundred and eighty million souls in all of India.

PASSEPARTOUT. All under British rule?

MR NAIDU. No. A significant portion is still free. Well, I've
business to attend to but I will see you both on the train.

FOGG. Indeed.

  MR NAIDU *exits*.

PASSEPARTOUT. The train?

FOGG. Yes, the recently completed Great Indian Peninsula
Railway. It will take us from Bombay to Calcutta in three
days' time.

PASSEPARTOUT. Are you to see the sights first, Mr Fogg?

FOGG. No.

PASSEPARTOUT. But I've heard it is a fascinating city!
Bazaars, mosques, and the noble temple on Malabar Hill?
Wouldn't you like to see *that*, sir?

FOGG. It seems like you would.

PASSEPARTOUT (*he would*). No. No. (*A thought.*) Unless you
would like me to see it *for* you? Bring you a full report, sir?

FOGG. I will have our passports stamped. Please make the
usual purchases. The rest of the day is yours to do as you
will. We depart at exactly eight p.m. I'll see you at the train.

PASSEPARTOUT. Thank you, sir.

FOGG *walks off.* PASSEPARTOUT *wanders into the bazaar. Nearby,* FIX *berates the* BOMBAY CONSUL.

FIX. No warrant from London, you say? Nothing?!

BOMBAY CONSUL. No, Inspector.

FIX. Well, then, I must keep them here until it arrives! They must not board that train!

FIX *makes his way through the bazaar until he finds* PASSEPARTOUT.

Oh, Mr Passepartout!

PASSEPARTOUT. Why, *Monsieur* Fix! Taking in the sights?

FIX. Yes, so much to see! In fact, the temple on Malabar Hill is just up the road!

FIX *points and* PASSEPARTOUT *is drawn immediately to the temple in the distance.*

PASSEPARTOUT. Oh. It *is* beautiful!

FIX. But, we must watch the time. We wouldn't want Mr Fogg to leave without you!

PASSEPARTOUT. He would never leave without me!

FIX. Good! But, still, just a quick look.

FIX *leads* PASSEPARTOUT *to the temple.*
PASSEPARTOUT *enters and is totally engrossed.*

PASSEPARTOUT. *C'est magnifique!* Just look at the ceiling! I have never seen such –

Suddenly, PASSEPARTOUT *is jumped upon by three* ENRAGED MEN. *They fall upon him, tear off his shoes and begin to beat him with loud exclamations.*

FIX (*with delight, to himself*). Oh, yes! I forgot to mention, you must never enter the Malabar Temple with your *shoes* on!

PASSEPARTOUT *struggles to get away.*

Such a transgression results in a severe punishment!

In an amazing display of physical skill, PASSEPARTOUT, *now shoe-less, breaks away from the* MEN.

(*Lost in his glee.*) Having broken a law like that, you'll be arrested and tried! You won't be able to leave Bombay for days! Maybe weeks!

FIX *turns and realises* PASSEPARTOUT *has escaped.*

Aaaaagh!! (*Gathering himself.*) No! No! You'll not get away from me so easy as that, Mr Fogg! I will see you in Calcutta!

Transition: the boat on the map is replaced by a train.

Scene Ten

On the Way to Calcutta

FOGG *is playing cards with* MR NAIDU *on the train.* PASSEPARTOUT, *still shoe-less, sleeps with a little blanket over him.* MR NAIDU *glances at* PASSEPARTOUT.

MR NAIDU. You are lucky, Mr Fogg.

FOGG. How is that, Mr Naidu?

MR NAIDU. If Passepartout had been caught for not taking off his shoes in the temple, you would have met with a significant delay. Your Government takes a very serious view, and rightly so, of disrespect towards the religious practices of the Indian people.

FOGG. Mr Naidu, if he had been caught, he would have been condemned, punished, and quietly returned to Europe. I don't see how it would have delayed me.

MR NAIDU. I see. (*Glancing out of the train window.*) When I was a boy, the railway stopped at the base of these mountains. We were obliged to cross on ponies to the other side. Never did I imagine the train would one day climb the mountains, too. The world is surprising, isn't it, Mr Fogg?

FOGG. That all depends on what one is expecting, Mr Naidu.

MR NAIDU. And what do you expect of the world, Mr Fogg?

FOGG. Only that it can be travelled in eighty days.

MR NAIDU. Does nothing hold interest for you?

FOGG. Anything that can't be found in the *Bradshaw* isn't of much interest or expectation to me. (*Laying down cards.*) Hearts are trumps.

The train begins to slow. PASSEPARTOUT *wakes up.*

MR NAIDU. Why are we slowing? We aren't nearly there yet.

FOGG *gets up and looks out of the window.*

What time have you, Passepartout?

PASSEPARTOUT. Four in the afternoon.

MR NAIDU. Four? That can't be right. You must be hours slow. Haven't you regulated your watch?

PASSEPARTOUT. No. London time it shall stay!

MR NAIDU. But travelling eastward, the days are shorter by four minutes for each degree you pass. You will just keep falling further and further behind.

The train screeches to a halt.

PENINSULA CONDUCTOR (*offstage, in Hindi*). *Yātriyōṁ kō yahāṁ sē bāhara hō jā'ēgā!* [Passengers will get out here!]

PASSEPARTOUT. Where are we?

MR NAIDU *looks out of the window.*

MR NAIDU. In a forest of date and acacia trees, it seems.

The PENINSULA CONDUCTOR *steps into the car.*

PENINSULA CONDUCTOR. Passengers will get out here!

MR NAIDU. Get out? But why?

PENINSULA CONDUCTOR. The railway isn't finished.

PASSEPARTOUT. What!? Not finished?!

PENINSULA CONDUCTOR. Fifty miles of track is still to be laid from here to Allahabad.

The MEN *step off the train.*

PASSEPARTOUT. *Zut alors!* There is no more track?!

MR NAIDU. But the newspapers in Bombay announced last *month* that the railway had been completed!

FOGG. The London papers as well.

PENINSULA CONDUCTOR. They were mistaken.

PASSEPARTOUT. And yet you sell tickets from Bombay to Calcutta!

PENINSULA CONDUCTOR. Certainly, but the local passengers know that they must find transport themselves from here to Allahabad.

PASSEPARTOUT. But how are we supposed to get to – !

FOGG. Don't distress yourself, Passepartout, we will find a way to get there.

Scene Eleven

The End of the Line

FOGG *looks around calmly.*

FOGG. I have read in the *Journal of the Royal Geographical Society* that the Indian terrain can be crossed, with the speed and efficiency comparable to that of more advanced modes of transport, by a variety of four-legged creatures. The *Journal* states quite emphatically that with a local guide who knows the way, the journey can be made in equal time to that of a locomotive.

MR NAIDU. Well, your journal may be right theoretically, Mr Fogg, but procuring such an animal will be difficult as they are very valuable to their owners. We can certainly try, but in order to succeed, fortune must favour us.

MR NAIDU *and* PASSEPARTOUT *frantically ask passers-by for help with their transport, but to no avail.*

(*In Hindi.*) *Mujhē māpha karanā, kē li'ē apanē palki-gharis upalabdha hai – ?* [Excuse me, is your palki-gharis available to – ?]

PASSEPARTOUT. *Excusez-moi*, but is your pony – ?

MR NAIDU (*in Hindi.*) *Sara, yaha āpakē pālakī kirā'ē para karanē kē li'ē sambhava hai – ?* [Sir, is it possible to rent your palanquin – ?]

PASSEPARTOUT. Pardon me, but – Oh! Is that a zebra?! Never mind.

MR NAIDU. Excuse me, but – ?

PASSEPARTOUT. Excuse me, but – ?

MR NAIDU *walks over to* FOGG.

MR NAIDU. This is a delay greatly to your disadvantage.

FOGG. I have two days that I gained on *The Mongolia* to sacrifice. A steamer leaves Calcutta for Hong Kong at noon on the 25th. This is the 22nd. We shall be there in time.

PASSEPARTOUT *joins* FOGG *and* MR NAIDU.

PASSEPARTOUT. Everything seems to be taken, *monsieur*. Except...

An elephant arrives on stage, ridden by a local woman, MISS SINGH.

MR NAIDU. Let me see what I can do.

MR NAIDU *introduces himself to* MISS SINGH *and they have a brief exchange in the local language.* MR NAIDU *then crosses back to* FOGG.

This elephant is not trained for travel. He's to join the circus.

PASSEPARTOUT (*delighted*). The circus! (*Catching himself.*) Poor creature.

MR NAIDU. Miss Singh has been promised a great sum and she doesn't want to endanger the beast by taking this journey.

FOGG. Do you speak English, miss?

MISS SINGH. Yes, sir.

FOGG. I will pay you ten pounds an hour for the loan of him.

MISS SINGH. Not enough if something should happen.

FOGG. Twenty pounds?

MISS SINGH. No.

FOGG. Forty pounds?

MISS SINGH. No.

FOGG. I'll buy him from you then. What is the circus offering? A thousand pounds to buy the elephant.

MISS SINGH. Uh… no.

MR NAIDU (*quietly to* FOGG). Please, Mr Fogg, think carefully before you go any further. She will take you for all you are worth if you let her.

FOGG. Believe me, Mr Naidu, I am not in the habit of acting rashly, but a bet of twenty thousand pounds is at stake and the elephant has become absolutely necessary. (*To* MISS SINGH.) Twelve hundred?

MISS SINGH. No.

FOGG. Fifteen hundred?

MISS SINGH. No.

FOGG. Two thousand pounds.

PASSEPARTOUT. *Sacrebleu!*

MISS SINGH (*after a quick beat*) All right. Come along.

They all board the elephant.

We will go through the forest. Much faster that way.

MR NAIDU. Excuse me, isn't there a violent sect that lives in these forests?

MISS SINGH. Oh, they're not so bad. And anyway, it's dark. They won't see us. Probably.

Transition: the train is replaced by an elephant on the map.

Scene Twelve

Phileas Fogg Proves He Has Feelings After All

The group makes their way through the forest. In the distance, they see a beautiful woman, MRS AOUDA, *escorted by two* GUARDS.

PASSEPARTOUT. What is this?

MISS SINGH. A suttee.

PASSEPARTOUT. A suttee?

MR NAIDU. They are leading that widow to her husband's funeral pyre where she will die next to him.

PASSEPARTOUT. Poor girl!

MR NAIDU. The sacrifice is voluntary.

MISS SINGH. This one is not. Her name is Kamana Aouda –

MR NAIDU. No! Not *the* Kamana Aouda! Her sad story has filled the papers for weeks! (*Explaining to* FOGG.) She is the well-educated daughter of a wealthy Bombay merchant. When her father died, her uncle set out to claim his fortune by marrying her off to an old Rajah from this sect, knowing this fate awaited her.

MISS SINGH. She tried to escape but couldn't get away.

MR NAIDU. It's tragic.

PASSEPARTOUT. This cannot happen!

FOGG. Well... suppose we save her.

MR NAIDU. Save her?! Why, Fogg, you *do* have feelings after all!

FOGG. When I have the time.

MISS SINGH. We risk our lives if we are taken.

FOGG. So be it. We can create a diversion with the elephant.

The group confers for a moment and then they begin the plan.

Big Number – 'An Elephant Chase': the elephant 'rears' in some way, catching the attention of the GUARDS. *The* GUARDS *move in on the elephant. Just then,* PASSEPARTOUT *charges them, displaying his incredible fighting skill. As the* GUARDS *fight* PASSEPARTOUT, FOGG *quietly dismounts the elephant, goes to* MRS AOUDA, *introduces himself and asks her if she'd like to join him. When she agrees, he escorts her onto the elephant. Just as* FOGG *and* MRS AOUDA *are safely on the elephant,* PASSEPARTOUT *swings up onto the elephant away from the* GUARDS.

PASSEPARTOUT (*to* MISS SINGH). Go, *mademoiselle*! Don't stop until we have arrived in Allahabad!!

The elephant 'runs' away, leaving the GUARDS *behind.*

MR NAIDU. What a display, Passepartout!

FOGG. Yes, you are to be commended. (*Turning to* MRS AOUDA.) Mrs Aouda, I am Phileas Fogg. This is my valet, Passepartout, our travelling companion from Bombay, Mr Naidu and our guide, Miss Singh.

MRS AOUDA. I thank you, all of you, for rescuing me.

FOGG. I hope that you will you put aside any misgivings and trust me when I say that I will let no harm come to you.

MRS AOUDA. But, Mr...?

FOGG. Fogg.

MRS AOUDA. As long as I am on Indian soil, I am still hanging in the jaws of death, Mr Fogg.

FOGG. If you are willing, until you find a place of safety, I ask you to remain under my care and protection.

MRS AOUDA (*nodding*). Thank you.

MISS SINGH. Here we are. This is Allahabad.

The group disembarks the elephant.

FOGG. Miss Singh, the elephant is yours.

MISS SINGH. No, he is yours. You paid for him.

FOGG. The payment was for the elephant, not for the help you volunteered in the rescue. For that, you deserve to keep him.

MISS SINGH. Thank you, sir. The train station is just up that way. (*In Hindi.*) *Shubh kamnae!* [Good luck!]

The group bids MISS SINGH *goodbye. She departs with the elephant. The group makes their way to the train station, where they wait on the platform.*

FOGG. Mrs Aouda, this is Calcutta. Are you ready?

MRS AOUDA *nods, but turns away, obviously upset.*

MRS AOUDA. Yes, thank you.

FOGG. I regret if my offer has in any way displeased you.

MRS AOUDA (*with much heart*). No, I am humbled by your generosity. I am glad to live and graciously accept your offer, Mr Fogg. But you see… I accepted my death, no matter how bitterly I regretted it. And now, to be alive and forced to leave the home I love and all the many treasures in it? To never have my feet touch the soil of my country again…? To never hear the singing voices of my sisters or see the morning light on their children's faces as they grow up in our garden in Bombay…? You see, Mr Fogg, even with your generous offer, I can not yet look forward to the world beyond the one I have known – for it soon will be lost to me for ever.

FOGG. I see. Well, we will discuss everything when you've had more time to recover.

MRS AOUDA. Thank you, Mr Fogg.

MRS AOUDA *finally turns her eyes to* FOGG. *They hold eyes for a moment longer than expected.*

FOGG. Any Englishman would have done the same.

Transition: the elephant on the map is replaced by a train, and it continues its journey to Calcutta.

Scene Thirteen

Arrival in Calcutta

A train whistle. FOGG *and* PASSEPARTOUT *step out, followed by* MR NAIDU *and* MRS AOUDA.

FOGG. Arrival in Calcutta. 25th October. On schedule.

PASSEPARTOUT. You have lost your gain of two days, sir.

FOGG (*glancing at* MRS AOUDA). I do not regret it.

MR NAIDU. My business is here in Calcutta. So, I bid you farewell, my friends. Mr Fogg, I wish you all success and hope you will come though India again in a less original but more profitable fashion.

FOGG. Indeed.

   MR NAIDU *and* FOGG *shake hands.* MRS AOUDA *steps forward.*

MR NAIDU. When I return to Bombay, I will send word of your rescue to your sisters and news of your intent to live with your cousin in Hong Kong.

MRS AOUDA. I am more grateful than you can know, Mr Naidu.

MR NAIDU. Stay out of trouble, if you can, Passepartout.

PASSEPARTOUT. Of course, *monsieur*!

MR NAIDU (*to them all*). I wish you all a long and happy life! (*In Hindi.*) *Shubh kamnae!* [Good luck!]

   MR NAIDU *exits. Just out of the shadows,* FIX *appears. He points out* FOGG *and* PASSEPARTOUT *to a* CALCUTTA POLICEMAN, *who nods.* FIX *recedes back into the shadows. The* CALCUTTA POLICEMAN *watches* FOGG *and* PASSEPARTOUT *intently.*

FOGG. Our ship, *The Rangoon*, sails for Hong Kong in five hours. First, Passepartout, please send the telegram to Mrs Aouda's cousin so he knows to expect her when we arrive. After you've had the passports stamped and made the purchases, your time is your own.

PASSEPARTOUT. Very good, *monsieur*!

FOGG. And buy yourself some shoes.

PASSEPARTOUT. *Merci!*

    PASSEPARTOUT *exits*.

MRS AOUDA. Would you like to see a few of the sights here in Calcutta, Mr Fogg?

FOGG. If you care to, Mrs Aouda, I will certainly accompany you.

    They begin to walk off when the CALCUTTA POLICEMAN *approaches them, with* PASSEPARTOUT *in hand*.

CALCUTTA POLICEMAN. Mr Phileas Fogg?

FOGG. I am he.

CALCUTTA POLICEMAN. You are under arrest.

FOGG (*unfazed*). Very well.

CALCUTTA POLICEMAN. Be so good as to follow me.

    The group follows the the CALCUTTA POLICEMAN, PASSEPARTOUT *and* MRS AOUDA *are shocked*.

MRS AOUDA (*quietly to* FOGG *alone*). Mr Fogg, you have been arrested for having saved me!

FOGG. Quite impossible. News of your escape will not have reached here in this amount of time. I will escort you to Hong Kong as I gave you my word.

Scene Fourteen

The Trial

MRS AOUDA, FOGG *and* PASSEPARTOUT *are led to a courtroom.* JUDGE OBADIAH, *a fat, round man, enters, followed by a* CLERK.

CLERK. The first case – Phileas Fogg and his valet, Mr Passepartout.

JUDGE OBADIAH. For the last two days, the police have been looking for you on every train and boat from Bombay.

FOGG. We were slightly, but not fatally, delayed.

PASSEPARTOUT. But what are we accused of? Certainly saving this poor woman from a most horrible death can not be considered a –

The CLERK *produces* PASSEPARTOUT'*s shoes that he lost in the temple on Malabar Hill.* FIX *slinks out from the shadows.*

My shoes!

JUDGE OBADIAH. Your valet is charged with violating the sacred temple on Malabar Hill in Bombay on the 20th of October and as his employer you, too, must answer for it.

PASSEPARTOUT (*hanging his head, realising the arrest is his fault*). Oh no!

FOGG. Very well, your honour. I do.

JUDGE OBADIAH. You do?

FOGG. I do.

JUDGE OBADIAH. You mean, the facts are admitted?

FOGG. Admitted.

JUDGE OBADIAH. Well, then, that being the case, I sentence the said Passepartout and you, Mr Fogg, as his employer and the man responsible for him, to imprisonment for fifteen days.

FIX (*quietly to himself*). Yes!

FOGG. I see. Is there any circumstance in which you would forgo time served and instead allow us to pay a fine?

JUDGE OBADIAH. No circumstance.

FOGG. But, your honour, there is, is there not, the case of Barker vs. Watkins?

FIX (*quietly to himself*). What's this now?

FOGG. As I'm sure you remember, the case, convened in Singapore, was brought by a Mr Barker against the Honourable Judge Watkins on a charge of excessive punitivity. Its outcome set the precedent of allowing a fine to substitute for a sentence of time of twenty days or less.

JUDGE OBADIAH. Barker vs. Watkins, eh?

JUDGE OBADIAH *snaps his fingers and the* CLERK *scurries and brings him a gigantic law book that he thumbs through.*

FOGG. Of course, you'll remember, this only applies under certain criteria, including that the accused is in the employ of a British citizen who does not reside on the continent in which the alleged crime was to have been committed. Which is, in this circumstance, indeed, the case.

FIX (*panicked*). Can't be!

JUDGE OBADIAH. Yes, yes, here it is! Well, it certainly does set a precedent. Very well then, Mr Fogg. I am not certain I would do this for everyone, but your knowledge of obscure facts of British law has intrigued me. A fine of five hundred pounds, each, seems punishment enough.

FOGG. Thank you, your honour.

FIX (*to himself*). No!!

JUDGE OBADIAH. Next case!

FOGG *takes the roll of banknotes from the carpet bag and gives a couple to the* CLERK.

PASSEPARTOUT (*to the* CLERK). May I have my shoes back?

FOGG (*pulling* PASSEPARTOUT *along*). Passepartout.

MRS AOUDA, PASSEPARTOUT *and* FOGG *exit. FIX stares after them, stunned. The* CALCUTTA POLICEMAN *takes the shoes from the* CLERK *and offers them to* FIX.

CALCUTTA POLICEMAN. Sorry, Inspector. Would you like these?

FIX *takes the shoes, then throws them back at the* CALCUTTA POLICEMAN.

FIX. Send to Scotland Yard and tell them to forward the warrant for Mr Fogg's arrest on to Hong Kong. (*Looking after* FOGG.) If I fail, my reputation is lost and so is my reward. I must succeed in Hong Kong! To *The Rangoon*!!

The sound of a boat horn blowing.

Transition: a boat is placed on the map and it sets sail.

Scene Fifteen

On *The Rangoon*

MRS AOUDA *and* FOGG *sit on the deck having tea.*

Big Number – 'The Tea Dance': music plays as FOGG *and* MRS AOUDA *sit at a table drinking tea. The boat tips and their teacups slide off the table variously. They catch them and this becomes a playful dance as they sip a sip, lose their teacup, catch the other's, hand it back and begin again. This cycles through three times and is ended when the teacups are cleared by the* RANGOON PURSER.

MRS AOUDA. The waves are still quite strong. Last night, I thought I was to be forcibly thrown from my cabin! Did you sleep at all, Mr Fogg?

FOGG. I slept quite well.

MRS AOUDA. But we've slowed down so considerably and I know you must board a ship in Hong Kong no later than November 5th!

FOGG. I see that Passepartout has filled you in on the details of our journey.

MRS AOUDA. Now that I know, I am even more indebted to you.

FOGG. Nothing to be indebted for until I have left you safely with your cousin. As soon as we arrive, I will seek him out. Everything will be arranged with mathematical precision.

MRS AOUDA. The scenery is lovely, is it not? I sailed this route once with my father. We are near the Straits of Malacca.

FOGG. Indeed. The Straits link China, India and the Near East.

MRS AOUDA. It is so beautiful – the mountain on one side, the forest of bamboo on the other. Did you know that legend says it was discovered four hundred years ago by a brave Hindu Prince? Supposedly, he named the city after a malacca tree that had given him shelter during a storm.

FOGG. Malacca is at the centre of the maritime trade in this region and was an inevitable and logical result of its geography, regardless of who discovered it.

MRS AOUDA (*smiling at* FOGG). I suppose it was. Although I think I like the other story better, don't you?

FOGG. I do enjoy your perspective.

MRS AOUDA. And I yours.

FOGG. It is certainly… novel. (*Realising the time.*) For today, I must bid you *adieu*. Whist awaits. But tomorrow… shall we visit at the same hour we begin today?

MRS AOUDA. Yes, that should work out… with mathematical precision.

PASSEPARTOUT *runs up to them.*

PASSEPARTOUT. Mr Fogg! We have received word from *The Carnatic*!

FOGG. Yes?

PASSEPARTOUT. The ship took damage due to weather and will dock in Hong Kong for an additional twenty-four hours – we will make our connection!

MRS AOUDA. All this time, you thought you were to miss *The Carnatic*?! Oh, what if you did?

FOGG. There's no sense in worrying about what could have happened when it, indeed, has not.

MRS AOUDA (*struck by this*). I suppose you are right, Mr Fogg.

FOGG. Well... until tomorrow.

MRS AOUDA. Until tomorrow.

　FOGG *exits*.

　Passepartout, may I ask you something in confidence?

PASSEPARTOUT. *Mais oui*.

MRS AOUDA. Is Mr Fogg mathematical in *all* things?

PASSEPARTOUT. Yes, madam. I suppose he is.

MRS AOUDA (*after a moment*). I will retire to my cabin for a while. Thank you. For everything.

　PASSEPARTOUT *watches her go as* FIX *approaches him*.

FIX (*bad fake surprise*). What?! You here? On *The Rangoon*?!

PASSEPARTOUT. *Monsieur* Fix! I left you in Bombay and here you are on the way to Hong Kong! Are you going around the world, too?

FIX. No, no, I shall stop in Hong Kong – at least for some days. How is your Mr Fogg?

PASSEPARTOUT. As precise and punctual as ever. But, *Monsieur* Fix, you do not know that we now have a young lady with us.

FIX. How surprising! Come, Passepartout, tell me the whole story. They loaded some delicious gulab jamun in Calcutta. It's a dessert you won't soon forget!

PASSEPARTOUT. Well, perhaps a taste, if you insist!

　Transition: on the map, the boat arrives in Hong Kong.

Scene Sixteen

Arrival in Hong Kong

FOGG, MRS AOUDA *and* PASSEPARTOUT *arrive in Hong Kong.*

FOGG. Arrival in Hong Kong, Wednesday November 6th. Our ship, *The Carnatic*, departs for Yokohama tomorrow morning. We will stay here at the club hotel this evening. I'm off to seek Mrs Aouda's cousin.

MRS AOUDA. Thank you, Mr Fogg.

MRS AOUDA *walks into the hotel,* PASSEPARTOUT *and* FOGG *look after her.*

PASSEPARTOUT. I will miss her.

PASSEPARTOUT *looks to* FOGG, *who looks to the departing* MRS AOUDA.

Anything else, *monsieur*?

FOGG. Oh, no, thank you, Passepartout.

PASSEPARTOUT. Would you like to see the sights – ?

FOGG. Go ahead.

FOGG *heads out.* PASSEPARTOUT *looks around, getting caught up in the scenery, then pulls himself away to run his errand.*

Scene Seventeen

Hong Kong and Floating Gardens

MRS AOUDA *stands on a hotel balcony looking out at the city.* FOGG *enters.*

FOGG. Mrs Aouda, I have news of your cousin.

MRS AOUDA. Yes? Did you find him?

FOGG. No. He made an immense fortune here but quit this country two years ago. He now lives and works in Holland.

MRS AOUDA. Well... I wonder what I am to do now?

FOGG. Quite simple. Come with us to London and, from there, I will secure your safe passage to Holland.

MRS AOUDA. I thank you, Mr Fogg, but no. You have already done too much for me. I am not your responsibility. I am my own.

FOGG (*with difficulty, maybe for the first time in his life*). Yes, but... I cannot... rather, how will you... I mean, perhaps you would care to...

MRS AOUDA (*stunned by his stumbling*). Mr Fogg...?

FOGG (*recovered*). As you have never been to Europe before and do not know your way, it simply seems the most logical course of action that you join us.

MRS AOUDA (*teasing a little*). Oh, well, if it is the most *logical* course of action, I suppose that it's best.

FOGG (*oblivious to teasing*). Very well, then.

MRS AOUDA (*sad* FOGG *doesn't get the teasing*). Very well.

FOGG. Since we are bound for colder climes, I think it necessary we purchase you some travelling clothes.

MRS AOUDA. I suppose it is. But I shall keep track of your expenditures on me, Mr Fogg, and some day I will repay, if not your kindness, at least your pocket.

FOGG. I will have Passepartout engage an additional cabin aboard *The Carnatic* when he goes to have the passports stamped.

MRS AOUDA *nods in thanks and turns to look out at the view.*

MRS AOUDA. Have you seen the Canton River before?

FOGG. No, I have not.

MRS AOUDA. It is so different than what I imagined. There seem to be ships here from all nations.

FOGG. Yes, trading vessels, junks, sempas, tankas...

MRS AOUDA. And, look, the flower boats – like so many floating gardens.

FOGG. Yes, I suppose that is what they look like. Floating gardens. Hmm.

Scene Eighteen

Office of the Hong Kong Consul

FIX *talks with the* HONG KONG CONSUL *in the familiar British consul hat.*

HONG KONG CONSUL. Your warrant, Inspector, from London via Bombay.

FIX. Finally!

FIX *examines the warrant.*

It's expired!!

HONG KONG CONSUL. Oh. Hmm. I could send for another one, if you like.

FIX. Yes! Right away! But Fogg is about to leave Hong Kong and British soil. Once he does, I will have no authority over him at all! He must not leave Hong Kong!

PASSEPARTOUT *steps into the office with the passports.* FIX *tries to hide.*

PASSEPARTOUT. Excuse me, would you stamp these passports, please?

HONG KONG CONSUL. Absolutely.

PASSEPARTOUT *hands the* HONG KONG CONSUL *the passports, who stamps them.*

PASSEPARTOUT (*seeing* FIX *hiding badly*). *Monsieur* Fix!

FIX. Oh, Mr Passepartout! Getting your passport stamped, eh?

PASSEPARTOUT. *Oui, monsieur.* What are you doing here?

FIX. I'm just making some arrangements for my journey home.

PASSEPARTOUT. You haven't decided to go with us to America?

FIX. No. No.

The HONG KONG CONSUL *hands* PASSEPARTOUT *his passport.*

HONG KONG CONSUL. Here you are, sir. Enjoy your trip!

PASSEPARTOUT. Thank you. Well, goodbye, Mr Fix. It's been a pleasure.

PASSEPARTOUT *shakes* FIX*'s hand.*

FIX. Have you time to see Hong Kong?

PASSEPARTOUT. No! Our schedule has changed – *The Carnatic* is leaving tonight not tomorrow!

FIX. Leaving *tonight*, eh?

PASSEPARTOUT. *Oui.* I'm off to tell Mr Fogg.

FIX. Of course! We can't have Mr Fogg miss the boat! But before you go, wouldn't you like to stop in and see a local tavern? On me, of course, Mr Passepartout?

PASSEPARTOUT. Very kind of you, Fix, but I've seen enough taverns in my time. And I must tell Mr Fogg about *The Carnatic* –

FIX. But they have a most curious local tobacco that they smoke out of red clay pipes. You can't pass through Hong Kong without having tried it!

PASSEPARTOUT (*after looking at his watch*). There is time for a quick look, I suppose.

Scene Nineteen

Opium Den

FIX *and* PASSEPARTOUT *walk into a smoke-filled opium den. A few* OPIUM SMOKERS *lay around on pillows.* FIX *and* PASSEPARTOUT *sit at a little table with a pipe. They look around.*

FIX. Well, here we are.

FIX *hands* PASSEPARTOUT *a pipe.*

And here you go.

PASSEPARTOUT. Maybe just a small taste...

PASSEPARTOUT *takes a hit off the pipe and falls senseless upon the table.*

FIX. At last! I have Fogg once and for all!!

FIX *leaves the opium den. By sheer force of will,* PASSEPARTOUT *raises his head.*

PASSEPARTOUT (*out of it, trying to focus*). *The Carnatic*! Can't miss the boat! Can't miss *The Carnatic*!

PASSEPARTOUT *stumbles out of the opium den.*

Scene Twenty

The Next Morning at the Docks

MRS AOUDA, *wearing a new dress, and* FOGG, *holding the carpet bags, stand looking around the dock.*

MRS AOUDA. I was certain Passepartout would turn up this morning, here at the docks. Where could he have been all night?

FOGG. I left word of his disappearance and funds for his return home at the French consulate.

FIX *approaches them.*

FIX. Excuse me, did you intend to sail aboard *The Carnatic* this morning?

FOGG. Yes, sir.

FIX. So did I. I've only just learned it left last night without giving notice. We now must wait *a week* for another steamer.

MRS AOUDA. No! Oh, Mr Fogg!

FOGG (*evenly*). I seem to see some other vessels here in Hong Kong Harbour.

FOGG *approaches a ship's* CAPTAIN *coiling some line.*

Is your boat ready to sail?

CAPTAIN VON DARIUS. Yes, your honour.

FOGG. Are you the captain?

CAPTAIN BLOSSOM VON DARIUS *turns around. It is a woman.*

CAPTAIN VON DARIUS. Yes, Blossom Von Darius, Captain of *The Tankadere*.

FOGG (*taken aback by her gender*). Huh. (*Recovered.*) Does she go fast?

CAPTAIN VON DARIUS. Between eight and nine knots.

FOGG. Will you take me and my companion to Yokohama?

CAPTAIN VON DARIUS. Japan, man?! You must be joking!

FOGG. No. I must get there by the 14th at the latest to catch a boat for San Francisco.

CAPTAIN VON DARIUS. No! Out of the question – such a long journey with such a little boat? And at this time of year? She'd never make it in time!

FOGG. I promise you five hundred pounds if she does.

CAPTAIN VON DARIUS. But you can't promise calm seas and winds staying in the south-west, can you?

FOGG. No, I cannot.

CAPTAIN VON DARIUS. Then, it's impossible.

FOGG. Unlikely, perhaps, but not impossible.

CAPTAIN VON DARIUS. But you'd need perfect conditions and –

FOGG. Will you try? I will pay you… whatever the outcome.

CAPTAIN VON DARIUS. Whatever the outcome?

FOGG *holds out the five hundred pounds to* CAPTAIN VON DARIUS. *She takes them.*

We'll set sail in an hour or so.

FOGG. I will remind you, Captain, that time is of the essence.

CAPTAIN VON DARIUS. Half an hour then. But I don't think that's going to help.

CAPTAIN VON DARIUS *nods and readies the boat.*

FOGG. If you would like to join us, Mr –

FIX. Fix. Thank you, Mr –

FOGG. Fogg.

FIX. Fogg. I was about to ask the favour. But I will pay my own way.

FOGG. Let us not speak of that, sir.

FIX. But, I insist.

FOGG. No, sir. It enters into my general expenses.

They look out at the water.

MRS AOUDA. Poor Passepartout! Perhaps, in the confusion, he boarded *The Carnatic*?

FOGG. We will search for him in Yokohama before our boat sails for San Francisco.

MRS AOUDA. What if we don't find him? He has your passport!

FOGG. Please don't be alarmed. Things have a way of working themselves out.

Transition: Two boats are put on the map – The Carnatic (*large*) *and* The Tankadere (*small*).

Scene Twenty-One

Aboard *The Carnatic*

PASSEPARTOUT *stumbles out on the deck.*

PASSEPARTOUT (*stretches and yawns*). Ah! My head! (*Remembering.*) Oh! That Mr Fix! Tricking me like that! He has proved himself to be a meddler of some sort, for the gentleman of the Reform Club, I am sure, trying to sabotage Mr Fogg's journey! (*Remembering.*) At least I did not miss the steamer! But where is Mr Fogg?

The CARNATIC PURSER *walks by.*

Pardon me, have you seen Mr Fogg yet this morning?

CARNATIC PURSER. I don't believe there is a Mr Fogg on board.

PASSEPARTOUT. Surely he is! You might have seen him with some other gentleman playing whist...?

CARNATIC PURSER (*checking a passenger list*). I'm sorry, there is no Mr Fogg on board.

PASSEPARTOUT. No, he must be! And with him is Mrs Aouda...?

CARNATIC PURSER (*looking again at the list*). She is not on board either.

PASSEPARTOUT. But, it is impossible!

CARNATIC PURSER. Here is a passenger list. You may see for yourself.

PASSEPARTOUT (*scanning the list*). Am I on *The Carnatic*?

CARNATIC PURSER. Yes.

PASSEPARTOUT. On the way to Yokohama?

CARNATIC PURSER. Certainly.

PASSEPARTOUT. Yokohama, *Japan*?

CARNATIC PURSER. Of course! Now, if you'll excuse me…

The CARNATIC PURSER *walks away.*

PASSEPARTOUT (*stuck with the memory*). Oh, no! The bar! The smoke!! I forgot to tell Fogg!! He missed the boat! Fix!! The bet!! Ruin! And all my fault! All Passepartout! Oh, Mr Fogg! Mr Fogg!!!!

The ship's whistle blows.

End of Act One.

Entre-Act

Possibly during intermission, the circus arrives and there is some warming-up and practicing of circus tricks done in a comic, playful way.

ACT TWO

Scene Twenty-Two

Yokohama

Three CIRCUS PERFORMERS *warm up. In another area,*
PASSEPARTOUT *stands on a street corner, holding out his hat
and singing. A sign he carries reads 'Bound for America'.*

After a moment, the proprietor and ringmaster, the Honourable
WILLIAM BATULCAR, *American, stands right near the still
singing* PASSEPARTOUT *on the corner, and calls out to
passers-by.*

BATULCAR. Ladies and gentleman! Step right up! Don't miss
the last Yokohama appearance of Batulcar's Acrobatic
Troupe!

> BATULCAR *shouts over* PASSEPARTOUT*'s singing, so*
> PASSEPARTOUT *sings louder.*

(*Quietly to* PASSEPARTOUT.) Hey, shove off, this is my
corner.

PASSEPARTOUT. *Monsieur*, I am stranded and am trying to
make my way to America!

BATULCAR (*to the public again*). Final performance in the
Empire of the Sun before our tour of the States of the Union!

PASSEPARTOUT. You are bound for the United States?!

BATULCAR. That's right.

PASSEPARTOUT. I am – was – a circus man myself... are
there any openings?

BATULCAR. What can you do?

> PASSEPARTOUT *walks on his hands or does a flip,
> something physically impressive.*

PASSEPARTOUT. Trapeze, tightrope, tumbling and I can sing standing on my head, with a plate spinning on my left foot and a sabre balanced on my right.

BATULCAR. Good enough. You should fit the suit. Follow me.

BATULCAR leads him to the other CIRCUS PERFORMERS.

Here a man to replace Magnus. Luigi will show you. Follow him in everything.

PASSEPARTOUT *joins the other* CIRCUS PERFORMERS. *He is quickly dressed for the circus and* BATULCAR *introduces the act.*

And now, ladies and gentlemen, the attraction you all have been waiting for – for the last time in Yokohama before our tour of America, Batulcar's Acrobatic troupe – the best performers from around the globe! – perform the daring, the delightful, the death-defying… Human Pyramid! Prepare to be astonished by Batulcar's Acrobatic Troupe!!

Big Number – 'A Circus Act': lights and music. With much styling, the CIRCUS PERFORMERS *begin a human pyramid. At the height of the trick, shouting is suddenly heard and the* PERFORMERS *take a spectacular tumble.* PASSEPARTOUT, *the obvious cause of the tumble, has stepped out of the act. He approaches a couple sitting in the audience.*

PASSEPARTOUT. Is it you?! Is it *you*?!?!

The people he is talking to stand and are seen in the light. It is FOGG *and* MRS AOUDA*!*

FOGG. I thought I would find you here.

PASSEPARTOUT. But how…?!

FOGG. The weather was agreeable.

BATULCAR rushes over to them.

BATULCAR. You've ruined my act!

FOGG *give* BATULCAR *some money.*

FOGG. Sorry for the disturbance. Delightful show.

BATULCAR, *pacified, goes to check on his* PERFORMERS. FOGG *turns to* PASSEPARTOUT *and* MRS AOUDA.

Let us go! We've only moments to catch *The General Grant*!

Transition: a boat is placed on the map and it begins to sail from Japan to the USA.

Scene Twenty-Three

Aboard *The General Grant*

FOGG *and* MRS AOUDA *sit drinking tea out on the deck.*

Big Number – 'The Tea Dance' (Reprise): there is an abbreviated reprise of the tea dance. When it is over, the GENERAL GRANT PURSER *clears the teacups.*

FIX *watches* FOGG *and* MRS AOUDA *from afar.*

MRS AOUDA. Well, I am now certain that I care more about your success in this journey then you do, Mr Fogg.

FOGG. Why is that, Mrs Aouda?

MRS AOUDA. How can you remain so calm when we still have such a long way to go! And you have already used fifty-two of your eighty days!

FOGG. But the most difficult part of the journey is over. To this point, we were obliged to take an indirect route.

MRS AOUDA. Yes, certainly, the course *is* a straight one from here to Europe, but that doesn't mean it will go smoothly.

FOGG (*almost playfully*). Do you doubt me, Mrs Aouda?

MRS AOUDA. You're not the one I'm concerned about.

MRS AOUDA *looks to* PASSEPARTOUT, *who has joined them on the deck and looks up at the stars.*

PASSEPARTOUT. Oh! Orion is so bright tonight! (*Catching himself.*) Not that that's interesting. Everyone's seen Orion a hundred times. But, tonight…

PASSEPARTOUT *senses both* FOGG *and* MRS AOUDA *looking at him and he looks back at them.* PASSEPARTOUT *discreetly checks his teeth, his nose, etc.*

Is there something…?

FOGG *and* MRS AOUDA *share a smile.* PASSEPARTOUT *looks at his watch.*

(*Alarmed.*) Oh! Mr Fogg! The time!

The moment breaks between MRS AOUDA *and* FOGG.

FOGG. Oh, yes, of course. Time for bed. Goodnight.

MRS AOUDA. Goodnight.

FOGG *goes.* MRS AOUDA *looks after him for a moment.* FIX *sneaks over to listen in on* PASSEPARTOUT *and* MRS AOUDA.

So, it's eleven then, is it, Passepartout?

PASSEPARTOUT. Ten fifty-nine.

MRS AOUDA. Do you know, Passepartout, if your watch told both a.m. and p.m. you would see that we are now a full twelve hours ahead of London time.

PASSEPARTOUT. Impossible!

MRS AOUDA. It's true. For as of today, you and Mr Fogg have travelled exactly half the globe, so your watch is exactly twelve hours behind.

PASSEPARTOUT (*marvelling at this*). Half the globe…

PASSEPARTOUT *is back staring at the stars, lost in them.*

MRS AOUDA. I hope you'll get some rest tonight, Passepartout.

PASSEPARTOUT. Of course. Nothing to see here…

PASSEPARTOUT *does not move.*

MRS AOUDA. Goodnight.

MRS AOUDA *goes*. FIX *tries to sneak away, but*
PASSEPARTOUT *sees him*. PASSEPARTOUT *rushes* FIX,
much to the amusement of a group of PASSENGERS, *who*
immediately begin to bet on the fight that ensues.
PASSEPARTOUT *beats* FIX *soundly*.

FIX. Have you done?

PASSEPARTOUT. For the moment! But, you should know I
have figured out who you are, *Monsieur* Fix!

FIX. Well then, you should also know that if I succeed, I get
two thousand pounds. If you help me, I'll give you five
hundred of them.

PASSEPARTOUT. *Mon Dieu!* Now you try to bribe me?! When
we return – successfully! – to London, I intend to tell those
so-called gentleman at the Reform Club that sending you to
follow us was the most underhanded –

FIX. Hold on a tick… who do you think I am?

PASSEPARTOUT. A spy and a saboteur sent by the members of
the Reform Club, of course.

FIX. Listen to me. Passepartout, I am not who you think I am
and neither is your Mr Fogg. I am a police detective, sent by
Scotland Yard to find the thief of the Bank of England.

PASSEPARTOUT (*incredulous, laughing*). You are a detective?

FIX (*defensively*). Here is my commission.

FIX *hands a piece of paper to* PASSEPARTOUT, *who looks*
it over, not believing his eyes.

Mr Fogg's wager was only a ruse. You and the gentlemen of
the Reform Club are dupes. You see, Fogg is the thief of the
Bank of England!

PASSEPARTOUT. Impossible!

FIX. How can you be so sure? Just after the robbery, Fogg sets
off around the world on the most foolish pretext carrying
half of his considerable fortune rolled up in a carpet bag.

PASSEPARTOUT. *Monsieur* Fogg is the most honest of men!

FIX. Are you sure of that? Enough to be arrested as his accomplice?

PASSEPARTOUT. Even if it is true – which I can not believe – I will not interfere with his journey back to London for all the money in the world.

FIX. I don't want you to interfere. I want you to do everything you can to get Mr Fogg back on British soil.

PASSEPARTOUT (*confused, rubbing his head*). What?!

FIX. It is true I was trying to sabotage Mr Fogg's journey before but now I want him back in London as fast as possible.

PASSEPARTOUT. So you can arrest him for a crime he didn't commit?

FIX. The charge won't stick if he's as innocent as you say. In the meantime, I will do everything I can to help him. And it is only in England that we'll know for certain whether you are in the service of an honest man or a thief.

PASSEPARTOUT. But when we get back, you will let Mr Fogg finish his journey before you try to arrest him?

FIX. If he is, indeed, the honourable man you think he is.

FIX holds out his hand to PASSEPARTOUT.

Are we friends, then?

PASSEPARTOUT. Friends? No. Allies, perhaps.

FIX. Not a word to Fogg.

PASSEPARTOUT. *Oui*. But at the least sign of treason…

PASSEPARTOUT *holds up a fist.*

FIX. Agreed.

They shake hands.

Transition: the boat is replaced by a train that speeds across the plains.

Scene Twenty-Four

On the Train Across the Plains

FOGG, MRS AOUDA *and* PASSEPARTOUT *step into the light.*

FOGG. Arrival San Francisco, US of A. The train for Chicago departs momentarily.

> FOGG, MRS AOUDA *and* PASSEPARTOUT *move to a train car. They play cards.*

> From ocean to ocean, they say. In the past, the journey from San Francisco to New York under the most favourable conditions was at least six months, now it is just seven days.

MRS AOUDA. To think that this land, too, might still be under British influence if the Americans hadn't fought for their independence.

FOGG. British influence is not necessarily a bad thing, Mrs Aouda.

MRS AOUDA. For many people whose countries are no longer their own, it is indeed a bad thing, Mr Fogg.

> FOGG *takes that in.*

> But what I cannot figure out, putting aside one's ability to understand why the world must be conquered at all, is why the English need to remake everything in their own image... the language, the names, the buildings, the shops, making every place, the whole world, the same.

> FOGG *looks at her, taking that in.*

FOGG. Perhaps we just don't know how to see things any other way.

> FIX, *trying, but failing, to inconspicuously read a newspaper, cannot contain an enormous sneeze which echoes through the train car.* FOGG *looks to him.*

> Why, Mr Fix!

FIX (*bad fake surprise*). Mr Fogg!

FOGG. Is it possible we crossed the Pacific together and did not meet again on the steamer?

MRS AOUDA. And now we find you with us on the way to America aboard not only the same train, but the very same car?

FIX. Yes, well, my plans changed and now I am headed back to England myself.

FOGG. Well, you must join our party.

FIX. Oh, I couldn't. I already owe you so much, Mr Fogg.

FOGG. Nonsense. I have now successfully taught Mrs Aouda and my valet Passepartout –

FIX. Oh… hello.

PASSEPARTOUT. *Bonjour*, Mr Fix.

FOGG. – how to play whist. With you along, we will be able to play in earnest.

FIX. Well, I would certainly be delighted to continue the journey in such pleasant company.

FIX *looks to* PASSEPARTOUT, *who looks ready to hit him at any moment.* FIX *joins them.* FOGG *deals cards.*

MRS AOUDA. Look there!

They all look out of the window.

It's buffalo! A herd of buffalo! There must be a thousand!

FOGG. Looks like several thousand.

MRS AOUDA. Isn't that magnificent!

PASSEPARTOUT. They are so close!

MRS AOUDA. What if they want to cross the tracks?

FOGG. I have read in the *Journal of the Royal Geographical Society* that if a single buffalo decides to cross them, all will follow. Thousands of them will pass over for hours with nothing for us to do but wait.

MRS AOUDA. No!

PASSEPARTOUT, MRS AOUDA *and* FIX *look at each other nervously at this news.*

PASSEPARTOUT. What a country! Mere cattle stopping the trains! *Parbleu!*

FIX. But surely, Mr Fogg, such a thing is unlikely.

FOGG. It is dependant on the will of the animal, so it is altogether impossible to say.

Suddenly, a man, COLONEL STAMP PROCTOR, *appears behind them.*

COLONEL STAMP PROCTOR. I'd play a diamond.

FOGG, MRS AOUDA, PASSEPARTOUT *and* FIX *raise their heads. They look to the well-dressed American behind them.*

FOGG. That may be the case, sir, but this is not your game and I would ask you to kindly refrain from commenting on mine.

COLONEL STAMP PROCTOR. What are you, an Englishman?

FOGG. Yes, I *am* an Englishman, Mr – ?

COLONEL STAMP PROCTOR. The name's Colonel Stamp Proctor. And you are?

FOGG. Phileas Fogg.

COLONEL STAMP PROCTOR. It's no surprise then! Of course, with a hand like that, an Englishman would think of playing a club!

FOGG throws down his card.

FOGG. Not only think it, but play it!

COLONEL STAMP PROCTOR. You don't understand anything about whist, Limey!

FOGG stands.

FOGG. Perhaps I'll be better at another game, Yankee!

COLONEL STAMP PROCTOR. Oh yeah?!

FOGG. It would not be right for an Englishman to permit himself to be treated this way without retaliating.

COLONEL STAMP PROCTOR. A duel, you mean?

FOGG. Indeed, sir.

COLONEL STAMP PROCTOR. You just name the time and place!

FOGG. Presently, I am in a great hurry to get back to Europe but will you agree to a meeting in six months' time?

COLONEL STAMP PROCTOR. Six months!? Why not ten years?

FOGG. I say six months and I shall be at the meeting place exactly on time!

COLONEL STAMP PROCTOR. Now or never!

Cries and gunshots are heard. The TRAIN PORTER *rushes into the car.*

TRAIN PORTER. It's an ambush! Get down, everyone! If the bandits board – fight for your lives!!

Big Number – 'Bandits Attack the Train': the train is attacked by BANDITS. *In a remarkable show of strength and courage and skill far surpassing what* PASSEPARTOUT *has shown before, he beats off all the* BANDITS *and keeps everyone from harm. Just as he is being congratulated, an unseen* BANDIT *grabs* PASSEPARTOUT *and drags him away at gunpoint.*

PASSEPARTOUT (*as he is dragged away*). *Je suis désolé.* I'm sorry, Mr Fogg.

Scene Twenty-Five

In Which Phileas Fogg Simply Does His Duty

FOGG, MRS AOUDA, FIX *and* COLONEL STAMP PROCTOR *stand in the train car looking off after* PASSEPARTOUT.

MRS AOUDA (*through tears*). Oh, poor Passepartout!

FOGG. I will go after him.

FIX. But New York, the boat –

FOGG. It is my duty. Colonel – there comes a time when men must put aside their differences in pursuit of a greater good.

COLONEL STAMP PROCTOR. I agree with you, Fogg.

FOGG. Colonel, that man is my valet.

COLONEL STAMP PROCTOR. Well, there's a fort nearby and I know the commander. He'll let us borrow a few men for the job, I reckon.

FOGG. Very well. Let us waste no time.

FIX. Will you let me go with you?

FOGG. If you wish to do me a favour, you will remain with Mrs Aouda. In case anything should happen to me, I would ask you to escort her to Europe –

MRS AOUDA (*quoting* FOGG). There's no sense in worrying about something that has yet to come to pass.

FOGG (*getting it, almost a smile*). And, yet...

FOGG *and* MRS AOUDA *share a moment*.

FIX. Of course, I will stay.

MRS AOUDA. We will be waiting here on your safe return.

FIX. Good luck, Fogg.

FOGG *and* COLONEL STAMP PROCTOR *walk off.* FIX *and* MRS AOUDA *watch them go. The* TRAIN PORTER *walks through the car.*

TRAIN PORTER. There was little damage done to the train so we'll be on our way in an hour or so.

MRS AOUDA. But it will wait for them to come back – ?

TRAIN PORTER. We can't. We're already three hours late.

MRS AOUDA. When will another train pass here?

TRAIN PORTER. Tomorrow evening, ma'am.

The TRAIN PORTER *goes.* MRS AOUDA *fights back tears.*

MRS AOUDA. Tomorrow? Oh no, Mr Fix!

FIX. Try not to worry, Mrs Aouda, if anyone can figure their way out of this, it's Fogg.

Scene Twenty-Six

On the Platform

It is cold and snow falls. MRS AOUDA *stands on the train platform, looking out for* FOGG. FIX *waits a little way off from her. A man,* MR MUDGE, *approaches* FIX. *They talk quietly and* MR MUDGE *goes away.*

In the distance, a gunshot is heard. Out of the shadows emerges FOGG *and* COLONEL STAMP PROCTOR.

MRS AOUDA. And Passepartout?

PASSEPARTOUT *emerges.*

PASSEPARTOUT. *Bonjour, mademoiselle!*

MRS AOUDA. All in one piece?!

PASSEPARTOUT. In one piece!

COLONEL STAMP PROCTOR. Barely, but here he is. Well, we did it Fogg, didn't we?

FOGG. Indeed, Colonel. Indeed.

FIX. Well done, Fogg.

FOGG. Thank you, Mr Fix.

COLONEL STAMP PROCTOR. Where's the train?

FIX. Gone.

MRS AOUDA. The next one will come tomorrow.

FOGG (*evenly*). Ah. The *Bradshaw*.

PASSEPARTOUT. I have ruined you!

COLONEL STAMP PROCTOR. I wish I could help ya'll.

FOGG. You have been help enough for a lifetime, Colonel.

COLONEL STAMP PROCTOR. Well, I sure do hope the way
    we put aside our petty slights for the common good serves as
    an example of the way real men should behave.

FOGG. An attack on a man's honour is not just a 'petty slight',
    Colonel, but you are right that –

COLONEL STAMP PROCTOR (*getting into it*). Hey now,
    Fogg, you're not suggesting that –

FOGG (*back at him with restraint*). No, Colonel, I don't
    suggest, I mean it plainly that –

COLONEL STAMP PROCTOR (*fully in it now*). Maybe we
    should settle this, right now, once and for all –

FOGG. An excellent idea –

MRS AOUDA. Gentleman! Mr Fogg! The journey!

FOGG. Oh, yes, of course.

COLONEL STAMP PROCTOR. Well, goodbye then, Fogg. I
    hope our paths never cross again here or anywhere else.

FOGG. Fare you well, Colonel. And I share your hopes exactly.

They shake hands formally and COLONEL STAMP
    PROCTOR *exits*.

MRS AOUDA. Oh, we are hours behind!

FIX. Weren't we to change trains in Chicago?

MRS AOUDA. Yes, but we'll never make the connection now!
    Oh, we must be in New York before eight o'clock on the 11th!

PASSEPARTOUT. To catch steamer for Liverpool!

MRS AOUDA. But how?

PASSEPARTOUT. What about a balloon?

MRS AOUDA. A balloon?!

PASSEPARTOUT. *Oui!* A hot-air balloon! Is there a schedule for such a thing in the *Bradshaw*?

FOGG. No, Passepartout, there are no balloons in the *Bradshaw*.

PASSEPARTOUT. Are you certain, sir? I think I remember seeing a picture of one somewhere. A big striped one, I think… it was red and white…

FOGG. I'm telling you, no matter how carefully you look – (*Out to the audience.*) there is *no balloon in the book.*

FIX. What about a sledge?

MRS AOUDA. A what?

FIX. A sled… with sails. A *sledge* they call it. A man called Mudge has one and proposed such a method to me when he saw that we were stranded by the train.

PASSEPARTOUT (*very intrigued*). A sledge?!

FIX. In winter, he says, they slip over the surface of the frozen prairies with a speed superior to that of the express trains.

PASSEPARTOUT (*delighted, to* FOGG). Your decision to travel in winter will now work to our advantage!

FOGG. Let us meet this Mr Mudge.

The group walks to MR MUDGE *and finds him with his amazing sledge. We see* FOGG *make a deal with* MR MUDGE *and the group gets in the sledge.*

The train on the map is replaced by a sledge.

Big Number – 'Sledge Ride': MR MUDGE *puts on his goggles. The group gets on and off the sledge goes, flying across the ice, the sail full of air. The wind blows, the metallic lashings vibrate making a beautiful, plaintive melody.* FOGG *and* MRS AOUDA *listen, their faces close to one another. The music rises and all sing a lovely melody in tune with the sledge.*

Transition: on the map, the sledge is replaced by a train that arrives in New York.

Scene Twenty-Seven

New York Dock

The group rushes to the dock.

PASSEPARTOUT. Oh, New York! If only we had time to see the sights.

FOGG (*evenly*). Passepartout.

PASSEPARTOUT (*reining himself in*). Yes, *monsieur*.

They see a SAILOR *winding a rope.*

FOGG. Pardon me, we are looking for a steamer called *The China*. It is bound for Liverpool.

SAILOR. You just missed her. You can still see her outline on the horizon.

The group looks out to sea, defeated, except for FOGG. *He takes out the* Bradshaw.

FOGG. Nothing directly to Liverpool until tomorrow night. Come along.

They walk and find another boat docked in the harbour. FOGG *approaches the captain,* CAPTAIN SPEEDY, *an old New England sailor in a raincoat and cap.*

Are you the captain?

CAPTAIN SPEEDY. I am. Andrew Speedy. Captain of *The Henrietta*. Who are you?

FOGG. I am Phileas Fogg. You are going to put out to sea?

CAPTAIN SPEEDY. In an hour.

FOGG. You are bound for – ?

CAPTAIN SPEEDY. Bordeaux.

FOGG. Will you carry me and three other persons –

CAPTAIN SPEEDY. No. No passengers. Never have passengers. Too much in the way.

FOGG. We are bound for Liverpool and –

CAPTAIN SPEEDY. Liverpool? Why not Timbuktu?! No. I'm setting out for Bordeaux and to Bordeaux I'll go.

FOGG. Will you carry us to Bordeaux, then?

CAPTAIN SPEEDY. Not if you paid me two hundred dollars.

FOGG. I offer you two thousand dollars.

CAPTAIN SPEEDY. Two thousand dollars?

FOGG. Each.

CAPTAIN SPEEDY. Two thousand? For each one of the four? (*Off* FOGG*'s nod.*) We set sail right away!

Transition: three HENRIETTA CREWMEN *appear and they sing a sea shanty as the boat is built.* FOGG *and* MRS AOUDA *both recognise the other is singing along and are surprised.*

MRS AOUDA. I used to sail with my father.

FOGG. As did I.

Transition: on the map, the train is replaced by a boat.

Scene Twenty-Eight

Aboard *The Henrietta*

MRS AOUDA, FIX *and* PASSEPARTOUT *stand on the deck. The captain, seen from the back in cap and raincoat, looks out to the water.*

MRS AOUDA. Do you think we will make it at this speed, Mr Fix?

FIX. Only one way to find out. (*To the captain.*) Captain Speedy, what time are we making?

The captain turns around and it is revealed to be FOGG *in captain's gear.*

FOGG. Between eleven and twelve knots.

MRS AOUDA. Mr Fogg! Where is Captain Speedy?

FOGG. Resting in his cabin under lock and key.

FIX. Whatever for, Fogg?

FOGG. The sailors on board were persuaded that Liverpool was as good a destination as Bordeaux, and since Mr Speedy was the only one not in agreement, he had to be relieved of his duties. (*Calling to the crew.*) Pawl the capstain! Keep your luff, men!

Thunder and a flash of lightning!

MRS AOUDA. Those clouds in the distance look awfully menacing.

Big Number – 'Storm at Sea': a sudden and short storm at sea sequence with lightning, thunder, snow, wind and much yelling of nautical terms. The storm ends as quickly as it began. FOGG *looks around.*

FOGG. Well, that was blustery. Everyone all right?

The group nods and an ENGINEER *approaches* FOGG.

ENGINEER. Captain, we had just enough coal to go *half steam* to Bordeaux, but it won't last going *full steam* to Liverpool.

FOGG. Do not let the fires go down. Keep them up to the last! Have Speedy brought to the deck.

ENGINEER. Aye, Capt'n.

The ENGINEER *calls down a hatch.*

Bring up Speedy!

FIX *looks nervously to* PASSEPARTOUT.

FIX. The storm has put us terribly behind. We'll never get there unless we can run full steam!

PASSEPARTOUT. If Mr Fogg can get us out of this one, he's one for the ages!

CAPTAIN SPEEDY *arrives on the deck.*

FOGG. I have sent for you, sir –

CAPTAIN SPEEDY. Pirate!

FOGG. I have sent to ask you –

CAPTAIN SPEEDY. Dog!

FOGG. Sir, to ask you –

CAPTAIN SPEEDY. Sea rover!

FOGG. To sell me your vessel for I am going to have to burn it.

CAPTAIN SPEEDY. Burn *The Henrietta*!?

FOGG. The upper part of her at least. For fuel. The coal has given out.

CAPTAIN SPEEDY. Burn a ship worth fifty thousand dollars!?

FOGG *reaches in his bag and pulls out some banknotes.*

FOGG. Here is the *equivalent* of sixty thousand dollars. It is yours in exchange for the ownership of *The Henrietta*.

FIX (*quietly to* PASSEPARTOUT). Look at Speedy! No true American can fail to be moved by the sight of sixty thousand dollars.

PASSEPARTOUT. Sixty thousand!?! But how? We only have four hundred left!

FIX. That's in *dollars*, which only works out to about to about... three hundred pounds. The dollar isn't what it used to be.

FOGG *hands* CAPTAIN SPEEDY *the banknotes.*

FOGG. Don't let this astonish you, sir. I must arrive in London by a quarter before nine on the evening of the 21st of December or lose all my means in this world. I missed the steamer in New York and as you refused to take me to Liverpool –

SPEEDY. And well I did – for I stand to gain quite a profit by it! Can I keep the iron hull?

FOGG. The iron hull and the engine. Is it agreed?

CAPTAIN SPEEDY. Agreed.

FOGG *and* CAPTAIN SPEEDY *shake.*

You know, Captain...?

FOGG. Fogg.

CAPTAIN SPEEDY. Captain Fogg, you've got something of the Yankee about you.

FOGG *calls to the crew.*

FOGG. Very well, now! Tear down the masts, the booms, the shrouds and the spreaders, and get them in the fire! Full steam ahead!

Everyone leaps into action.

MRS AOUDA. Will it be enough, do you think, Mr Fogg?

FOGG. Yes, Mrs Aouda...

FOGG *throws his walking cane down the hatch to the engine room.*

Just enough.

Transition: on the map, the boat arrives on English shore!

Scene Twenty-Nine

Liverpool

The group carries their luggage. FOGG *looks at his watch.*

FOGG. Arrival in Liverpool, England, 21st December. We are now only six hours from London. The next train leaves momentarily.

FIX *steps in front of them.*

FIX. Phileas Fogg, for the robbery of the sum of fifty-five thousand pounds from the Bank of England, I arrest you in the name of Her Majesty the Queen!

PASSEPARTOUT. He is innocent! And you promised you would –

FIX. I didn't follow an innocent man all the way around the world!

MRS AOUDA. Oh, Mr Fix! How could you take such advantage of Mr Fogg and now be responsible for his ruin?!

FIX. Just doing my job, ma'am.

FOGG. Clearly there has been a misunderstanding that we will sort out as quickly as possible.

FIX *leads them on. They enter the police station.*

LIVERPOOL POLICEMAN. Fix! We never thought we'd see you again!

FIX. Yes, well. Here I am. And not only me, but the robber of the Bank of England, Mr Phileas Fogg!

LIVERPOOL POLICEMAN. Phileas Fogg? Aren't you the bloke going round the world in eighty days?

FOGG. Yes, I am.

FIX. That was all a ploy to throw off the police! Phileas Fogg is the thief of the Bank of England?!

LIVERPOOL POLICEMAN. Oh, no! We caught him that did the Bank of England job three days ago off the Australian coast.

PASSEPARTOUT. I knew it!

FOGG *steps forward to punch* FIX. PASSEPARTOUT *holds him back.*

Please, allow me.

PASSEPARTOUT *steps forward to punch* FIX. MRS AOUDA *holds him back.*

MRS AOUDA. No, please, allow me!

MRS AOUDA *punches* FIX *hard in the nose.*

FOGG. Well hit!

FIX. Deserved that, really.

FOGG *looks admiringly at* MRS AOUDA.

MRS AOUDA. Shouldn't we go, Mr Fogg?

FOGG. Yes, of course!

PASSEPARTOUT. If we catch a train right away, we might still make it!

MRS AOUDA. Let us hurry!

FOGG. Indeed.

> FOGG, MRS AOUDA *and* PASSEPARTOUT *rush out of the police station.*

LIVERPOOL POLICEMAN (*calling after them*). I'm to make a tidy sum if you succeed!

FIX. Good luck, Fogg!

> *Transition: the train is placed on the map and it arrives in London.*

Scene Thirty

Home Again

MRS AOUDA *and* PASSEPARTOUT *run as fast as they can from the train station.*

MRS AOUDA. Hurry, Mr Fogg!

PASSEPARTOUT. You've barely any time!!

> PASSEPARTOUT *and* MRS AOUDA *realise* FOGG *isn't behind them. They turn and see him standing stock still looking at his watch.*

FOGG. No need to hurry, my friends. It is already…

> *A clock chimes nine.*

Nine o'clock. We are too late. We are moments too late.

PASSEPARTOUT (*the reality of their loss descending on him*). Mr Fogg, it is all my fault.

MRS AOUDA. No, it is mine –

FOGG. I blame no one.

They walk home dejectedly. They arrive at the house and enter. FOGG *puts away the* Bradshaw. PASSEPARTOUT *turns out his burning gas lamp, left on so many days before.*

Scene Thirty-One

Phileas Fogg Settles His Affairs

MRS AOUDA *sits in the drawing room.* PASSEPARTOUT *enters with a teapot and two teacups.*

MRS AOUDA. How is he?

PASSEPARTOUT. He seems to have slept a little. He spent the day in his office getting his affairs in order. He is coming down to speak with you directly.

MRS AOUDA. Do you know what he wishes to discuss?

PASSEPARTOUT. Probably the journey to your cousin in Holland.

MRS AOUDA. Probably.

FOGG *enters and sits opposite* MRS AOUDA.

FOGG. Good evening.

MRS AOUDA. Good evening.

PASSEPARTOUT *pours them each a cup of tea and begins to exit as* FOGG *takes a sip.*

FOGG (*stunned*). Passepartout, is this my regular tea?

PASSEPARTOUT. No, sir. I brought it back from Japan. I thought you might like it.

FOGG. Yes, well. (*Realising.*) It is rather good, I must say.

PASSEPARTOUT *begins to go.*

Passepartout, I will try and help you find another position, but I am no longer... I no longer have the opportunities I once did –

PASSEPARTOUT. Don't trouble yourself, *monsieur*. I will find my way to... something else. I always do. And you will find your way, too... for it is simply true that in this world, a man of your station has more opportunity on your worst day than a man of mine does on his best.

PASSEPARTOUT *turns to go*.

FOGG. I suppose you're right, Passepartout. (*After a moment*.) Thank you. For everything.

PASSEPARTOUT. You're most welcome, Mr Fogg.

FOGG *nods, humbled*. PASSEPARTOUT *exits*. FOGG *and* MRS AOUDA *sit in a charged silence for a moment*.

FOGG. When you came with me from your own country, I was a man of means. I counted on putting a portion of my fortune at your disposal so that your life could be free and happy. But now I am penniless and can offer you nothing. And so, I ask you to forgive me for bringing you to England.

MRS AOUDA. I ask you to forgive me for having joined you and delayed you and thus contributed to your ruin.

FOGG. No, circumstances were simply against me.

FOGG *reaches for a small purse of money*.

Still, I beg to place in your hands the little that remains.

MRS AOUDA. I beg you to keep it for yourself. For what will become of you, Mr Fogg?

FOGG. I need nothing.

MRS AOUDA. Your friends will certainly –

FOGG. I have no friends.

MRS AOUDA. Well, then, your relations will –

FOGG. I no longer have any relations.

MRS AOUDA. Well, then, Mr Fogg, we are two of a kind. I, forced from my family and my home, have also lost any means I had in this world. But the worst is not to be bereft of means but of loving companions; saddest of all is that we've no heart with which to share our grief, for even the worst misery, when shared by two sympathetic souls, is more than bearable.

FOGG. They say so.

Smiling, she slides a teacup in the direction of FOGG. *Out of habit, he catches it, but in a rare bit of awkwardness, he bobbles the cup and drops it to the floor. He goes to his knees to retrieve it.* MRS AOUDA *reaches out her hand.*

MRS AOUDA. Mr Fogg...

From the ground, FOGG *looks to her. In the first impulsive moment we have ever seen, he takes her hand and puts it to his cheek.*

Phileas, would you like a devoted companion to share all your griefs and all your happiness with? Would you like both a relative and a friend? Would you like as much as I would, for me to be your wife?

FOGG. Through your eyes I want to see the world – and by everything that is sacred in it, Kamana, I love you and am wholly yours!

She presses his hand to her heart. FOGG *stands and holds her in his arms.*

(*Calling.*) Passepartout! Passepartout!

PASSEPARTOUT *enters.*

If it is not too late, please go to the Reverend Wilson's and see if he will marry us...

PASSEPARTOUT (*delighted*). Marry?!?

FOGG *looks to* MRS AOUDA.

FOGG. Tomorrow?

MRS AOUDA. Yes, tomorrow!

PASSEPARTOUT. Right away!!

PASSEPARTOUT *sets off.*

Scene Thirty-Two

In Which Passepartout Learns What Time It Is

PASSEPARTOUT *rushes down the street past the* FLOWER-SELLER.

FLOWER-SELLER. Well, I'll be jiggered! You're back!

PASSEPARTOUT. No time! Must get to Reverend Wilson's!

FLOWER-SELLER. He's got no time for anyone now. He's his sermon to practise for tomorrow. How was your trip?

PASSEPARTOUT. Sermon? But tomorrow's Monday.

FLOWER-SELLER. Monday? No, tomorrow's Sunday!

PASSEPARTOUT. Sunday? What day is it??

FLOWER-SELLER. Why it's Saturday the 21st of December!

PASSEPARTOUT *looks to his watch and traces a finger backwards around the dial.*

PASSEPARTOUT (*realising*). Four minutes for each degree...! (*Dawning on him.*) It's Saturday!? (*Realisation.*) It's Saturday! (*Jubilation.*) It's *Saturday*!!!

PASSEPARTOUT *kisses the* FLOWER-SELLER *and frantically runs down the street.*

Mr Fogg – you did it! But there's only ten minutes to get to the Reform Club!! Mr Fogg! Mr Fogg!! Mr Fogg!!!

Scene Thirty-Three

Inside the Reform Club

STUART, RALPH *and* FLANAGAN *stand staring at the clock.*

RALPH. Less than one minute left!

STUART. Could you believe the crowd gathered outside? You'd think half of London was here to see Phileas Fogg *lose*!

FLANAGAN. Don't be too hasty. You know that Mr Fogg is very eccentric. I should not be surprised if he still appeared before us.

RALPH. Ten seconds!

STUART. Mr Fogg's project was absurdly foolish and bound from the first to fail! He has lost, gentlemen, he has a hundred times lost!

The MEN *watch the clock...*

STUART/RALPH/FLANAGAN. Five, four, three, two, one – !

FOGG (*calmly as if he never left*). Good evening, gentlemen.

FOGG *has arrived! The* MEN *look to him.*

Here I am.

Scene Thirty-Four

Wouldn't You?

Everyone gathers around FOGG *and* MRS AOUDA, *dressed for their wedding.* PASSEPARTOUT *talks to the* FLOWER-SELLER.

PASSEPARTOUT. So you see, because we travelled constantly eastward, towards the sun, we gained four minutes with each degree we crossed. Three hundred sixty degrees multiplied by four minutes is precisely twenty-four hours! And that is

how Mr Fogg gained a day and won his bet of twenty
thousand pounds!

FLOWER-SELLER. But how did Mr Fogg, as smart a
gentleman as he is, not think of that himself?

PASSEPARTOUT *looks to* MR *and* MRS FOGG.

PASSEPARTOUT. He was a little distracted, I think.

FLOWER-SELLER. So, you say, he spent twenty thousand
pounds to make the journey and only won twenty thousand
in the bet? What has he gained by all that trouble?

PASSEPARTOUT. No money was made, but he did what he
said he could, what he gave his word he would!

STREET-SWEEP. But he gained nothing else?

PASSEPARTOUT. Nothing but a beautiful and loving wife who
makes him the happiest of men. (*Out to the audience*.) And
for that, wouldn't you, too, go around the world?

The MEN *of the Reform Club heartily concur.*

FOGG. Passepartout! We must get home and pack our bags!

PASSEPARTOUT. Bags, sir?!

FOGG. We're off on our honeymoon, of course! I travelled the
world, but I haven't yet *seen* it!

PASSEPARTOUT (*delighted*). Certainly, Mr Fogg!

PASSEPARTOUT *takes the* Bradshaw *off the shelf.*

I hear the Pyramids are extraordinary this time of year!

MR *and* MRS FOGG *hold each other and look at the giant
map of the world, charting their journey.*

The sound of a train whistle.

The End.

www.nickhernbooks.co.uk

facebook.com/nickhernbooks

twitter.com/nickhernbooks